50 Chile Food Recipes for Home

By: Kelly Johnson

Table of Contents

- Pastel de Choclo
- Empanadas de Pino
- Cazuela
- Completo
- Asado
- Porotos Granados
- Pebre
- Charquicán
- Pastel de Jaiba
- Ensalada Chilena
- Caldillo de Congrio
- Sopaipillas
- Humitas
- Paila Marina
- Carbonada
- Pan Amasado
- Mote con Huesillos
- Chacarero
- Confit de Pato
- Chile en Nogada
- Arroz con Mariscos
- Merluza a la Plancha
- Tortilla de Papas
- Chorillana
- Tarta de Mariscos
- Empanadas de Queso
- Ceviche Chileno
- Tarta de Manzana
- Pan de Pascua
- Torta de Mil Hojas
- Lomo a lo Pobre
- Arroz con Pollo

- Zapallo Italiano Relleno
- Ensalada de Palta
- Puchero
- Sopaipillas Pasadas
- Relleno de Pavo
- Calzones Rotos
- Leche Asada
- Mote con Huesillos
- Pionono
- Salmón a la Parrilla
- Ensalada de Porotos
- Tarta de Dulce de Leche
- Pescado a la Macho
- Empanadas de Mariscos
- Fideos con Salsa de Tomate
- Lentejas con Chorizo
- Pan de Trigo
- Arrollado de Huaso

Pastel de Choclo

Ingredients

For the Filling:

- 1 lb (450 g) ground beef
- 1 onion, finely chopped
- 2 cloves garlic, minced
- 1 red bell pepper, finely chopped
- 1/2 cup black olives, sliced
- 1/2 cup hard-boiled eggs, chopped
- 1/2 cup raisins
- 1/2 tsp cumin
- 1/2 tsp paprika
- Salt and pepper to taste
- 1 tbsp vegetable oil

For the Corn Topping:

- 4 cups fresh or frozen corn kernels (about 4-5 cups)
- 1 cup milk
- 2 tbsp butter
- 2 tbsp sugar
- 1/4 cup basil leaves (fresh or dried)
- Salt and pepper to taste

Instructions

1. **Prepare the Filling:**
   - Heat vegetable oil in a large skillet over medium heat.
   - Add the chopped onion and garlic, cooking until softened.
   - Add the ground beef and cook until browned.
   - Stir in the red bell pepper, olives, hard-boiled eggs, raisins, cumin, paprika, salt, and pepper.
   - Cook for an additional 5-7 minutes, allowing the flavors to meld.
   - Set the meat mixture aside.
2. **Prepare the Corn Topping:**
   - In a food processor or blender, combine the corn kernels and milk. Blend until smooth.
   - Transfer the corn mixture to a saucepan and cook over medium heat.
   - Add the butter, sugar, basil, salt, and pepper. Stir frequently until the mixture thickens and becomes creamy, about 10-15 minutes.

3. **Assemble the Pastel de Choclo:**
    - Preheat your oven to 375°F (190°C).
    - Spread the meat mixture evenly in the bottom of a baking dish.
    - Spoon the corn topping over the meat, spreading it evenly.
    - Use a fork to create a few decorative lines or patterns on top of the corn layer.
4. **Bake:**
    - Place the baking dish in the preheated oven.
    - Bake for 30-40 minutes, or until the top is golden and the filling is bubbly.
5. **Serve:**
    - Allow the Pastel de Choclo to cool slightly before serving.
    - Enjoy it warm with a fresh salad or other side dishes.

This comforting dish is a staple in Chilean cuisine and showcases the vibrant flavors and textures of traditional Chilean cooking.

Pastel de Choclo

Ingredients

For the Meat Filling:

- 1 lb (450 g) ground beef
- 1 onion, finely chopped
- 2 cloves garlic, minced
- 1 red bell pepper, finely chopped
- 1/2 cup black olives, sliced
- 1/2 cup hard-boiled eggs, chopped
- 1/2 cup raisins
- 1 tsp ground cumin
- 1 tsp paprika
- Salt and pepper to taste
- 2 tbsp vegetable oil

For the Corn Topping:

- 4 cups fresh or frozen corn kernels (about 4-5 cups)
- 1 cup milk
- 2 tbsp butter
- 2 tbsp sugar
- 1/4 cup fresh basil, chopped (or 1 tsp dried basil)
- Salt and pepper to taste

Instructions

1. **Prepare the Meat Filling:**
    - Heat vegetable oil in a large skillet over medium heat.
    - Add chopped onion and garlic, and sauté until softened.
    - Add ground beef and cook until browned, breaking it up with a spoon.
    - Stir in the chopped red bell pepper, black olives, hard-boiled eggs, raisins, cumin, paprika, salt, and pepper.
    - Cook for an additional 5-7 minutes, mixing well, then remove from heat.
2. **Prepare the Corn Topping:**
    - In a food processor or blender, puree the corn kernels with the milk until smooth.
    - Transfer the corn mixture to a saucepan and cook over medium heat.
    - Add butter, sugar, basil, salt, and pepper.
    - Stir frequently until the mixture thickens and becomes creamy, about 10-15 minutes.
3. **Assemble the Pastel de Choclo:**

- Preheat your oven to 375°F (190°C).
- Spread the meat filling evenly in the bottom of a baking dish.
- Spoon the corn topping over the meat, spreading it evenly.
- Use a fork to create a few decorative lines or patterns on top.

4. **Bake:**
   - Place the baking dish in the preheated oven.
   - Bake for 30-40 minutes, or until the top is golden brown and the filling is bubbling.

5. **Serve:**
   - Let it cool slightly before serving.
   - Enjoy your Pastel de Choclo warm!

This dish is beloved in Chile for its comforting flavors and layered textures, making it a great choice for a hearty meal.

Empanadas de Pino

Ingredients

For the Filling:

- 1 lb (450 g) ground beef
- 1 onion, finely chopped
- 2 cloves garlic, minced
- 1/2 cup black olives, sliced
- 1/2 cup hard-boiled eggs, chopped
- 1/2 cup raisins
- 1 tsp ground cumin
- 1 tsp paprika
- Salt and pepper to taste
- 1 tbsp vegetable oil

For the Dough:

- 3 cups all-purpose flour
- 1/2 cup vegetable oil or melted butter
- 1 tsp salt
- 1 cup warm water (adjust as needed)

Instructions

1. **Prepare the Filling:**
     - Heat vegetable oil in a large skillet over medium heat.
     - Add the chopped onion and garlic, and sauté until softened.
     - Add ground beef and cook until browned, breaking it up with a spoon.
     - Stir in the black olives, hard-boiled eggs, raisins, cumin, paprika, salt, and pepper.
     - Cook for an additional 5-7 minutes, allowing flavors to meld. Remove from heat and let it cool.
2. **Prepare the Dough:**
     - In a large bowl, combine the flour and salt.
     - Add the vegetable oil (or melted butter) and mix until the mixture resembles coarse crumbs.
     - Gradually add warm water, mixing until the dough comes together. It should be soft but not sticky.
     - Knead the dough on a floured surface for a few minutes until smooth. Cover and let it rest for about 30 minutes.
3. **Assemble the Empanadas:**
     - Preheat your oven to 375°F (190°C).

- Divide the dough into 12-16 equal pieces and roll each piece into a circle about 6 inches (15 cm) in diameter.
- Place a spoonful of the meat filling in the center of each dough circle.
- Fold the dough over the filling to create a half-moon shape. Press the edges together to seal, crimping with a fork or pinching with your fingers.
- Place the empanadas on a baking sheet lined with parchment paper.

4. **Bake:**
    - Brush the empanadas with a beaten egg or milk for a golden finish.
    - Bake in the preheated oven for 25-30 minutes, or until the empanadas are golden brown and crispy.
5. **Serve:**
    - Let the empanadas cool slightly before serving.
    - Enjoy them warm as a snack or with a side salad!

Empanadas de Pino are a delicious and satisfying treat, perfect for gatherings or as a comforting meal.

Cazuela

Ingredients

- **For the Broth:**
    - 2 lbs (900 g) beef shank or bone-in beef stew meat
    - 1 onion, quartered
    - 2 cloves garlic, smashed
    - 2 carrots, peeled and halved
    - 2 celery stalks, halved
    - 1 bay leaf
    - 1 tsp dried oregano
    - Salt and pepper to taste
    - Water (enough to cover the meat and vegetables)
- **For the Stew:**
    - 2 tbsp vegetable oil
    - 1 onion, chopped
    - 2 cloves garlic, minced
    - 1 red bell pepper, chopped
    - 1 cup butternut squash or pumpkin, cubed
    - 2 large potatoes, peeled and cubed
    - 1 cup green beans or peas
    - 1/2 cup corn kernels (fresh, frozen, or canned)
    - 1 cup cooked rice (optional)
    - 1/2 cup fresh parsley, chopped (for garnish)

Instructions

1. **Prepare the Broth:**
    - In a large pot, combine the beef, onion, garlic, carrots, celery, bay leaf, oregano, salt, and pepper.
    - Add enough water to cover the ingredients.
    - Bring to a boil, then reduce heat to low and simmer for about 1.5 to 2 hours, or until the meat is tender and the broth is flavorful.
    - Remove the meat and vegetables from the pot. Discard the vegetables, shred or chop the meat, and return it to the pot. Skim off any excess fat from the broth.
2. **Prepare the Stew:**
    - Heat vegetable oil in a separate large pot or Dutch oven over medium heat.
    - Add chopped onion and minced garlic, cooking until softened.
    - Stir in the red bell pepper and cook for a few minutes.
    - Add the butternut squash (or pumpkin) and cook for another 5 minutes.
    - Pour the beef broth into the pot with the vegetables.

- Add the cubed potatoes, green beans (or peas), and corn.
- Bring to a boil, then reduce heat and simmer until the vegetables are tender, about 20-25 minutes.
3. **Combine and Serve:**
    - If using rice, add it to the pot during the last 5 minutes of cooking to heat through.
    - Adjust seasoning with salt and pepper to taste.
    - Garnish with fresh parsley before serving.
4. **Serve:**
    - Ladle the cazuela into bowls, ensuring each serving has a good amount of meat and vegetables.
    - Enjoy warm with crusty bread or a side salad if desired.

Cazuela is a versatile dish and can be adapted with different vegetables and meats based on your preferences. It's a great way to enjoy a comforting, home-cooked meal with rich, hearty flavors.

Completo

Ingredients

- **For the Hot Dogs:**
    - 4 hot dog sausages
    - 4 hot dog buns (preferably soft and slightly toasted)
- **For the Toppings:**
    - 1 cup mayonnaise
    - 1/2 cup ketchup
    - 1/2 cup mustard
    - 1 cup sauerkraut or shredded cabbage
    - 1 ripe avocado, sliced or mashed
    - 1/2 cup chopped tomatoes
    - 1/4 cup finely chopped onions
    - 1/4 cup sliced pickled jalapeños (optional)
    - 1/2 cup shredded cheese (optional, usually a mild cheese like cheddar)

Instructions

1. **Cook the Hot Dogs:**
    - **Grill or Pan-Fry:** Preheat your grill or a skillet over medium heat. Grill or pan-fry the hot dog sausages until they are cooked through and have a nice char, about 5-7 minutes.
    - **Boil (Alternative Method):** You can also boil the hot dogs in a pot of water for about 5 minutes, or until heated through.
2. **Prepare the Toppings:**
    - **Avocado:** If using sliced avocado, simply cut it into thin slices. For mashed avocado, scoop the avocado into a bowl and mash it with a fork.
    - **Cabbage/Sauerkraut:** If using sauerkraut, drain it well. If using shredded cabbage, you can lightly season it with a bit of vinegar, salt, and pepper.
    - **Tomatoes and Onions:** Chop the tomatoes and finely chop the onions. You can mix them together if you like.
    - **Cheese:** If using shredded cheese, have it ready for sprinkling.
3. **Assemble the Completo:**
    - **Toast the Buns:** Lightly toast the hot dog buns if desired.
    - **Add Condiments:** Spread a layer of mayonnaise on the bottom of each bun. Add ketchup and mustard to taste.
    - **Add Hot Dogs:** Place the cooked hot dog sausages into the buns.
    - **Layer Toppings:** Top the hot dogs with sauerkraut or shredded cabbage, mashed or sliced avocado, chopped tomatoes, onions, and pickled jalapeños (if using). Sprinkle shredded cheese on top if desired.

4. **Serve:**
   - **Enjoy Immediately:** Serve the completos immediately while they are warm and the toppings are fresh.

Tips:

- **Variations:** You can customize your Completo with additional toppings like relish, sauerkraut, or even a fried egg for extra flavor.
- **Presentation:** Completo is often enjoyed with a side of Chilean-style French fries or a simple salad.

Completo is a beloved street food in Chile and reflects the country's love for bold flavors and hearty fare. Enjoy your homemade Completo with all the traditional toppings!

Asado

Ingredients

- **For the Meat:**
    - 2-3 lbs (900 g - 1.4 kg) beef ribs or short ribs
    - 2 lbs (900 g) sausages (chorizo or longaniza)
    - 1-2 lbs (450 g - 900 g) flank steak or skirt steak (optional)
    - Salt and pepper to taste
- **For the Marinade (Optional):**
    - 1/4 cup olive oil
    - 2 cloves garlic, minced
    - 1 tbsp fresh rosemary or thyme, chopped (or 1 tsp dried)
    - 1 tbsp red wine vinegar
    - 1 tbsp soy sauce
    - 1 tsp paprika
    - 1 tsp ground cumin
    - Salt and pepper to taste
- **For Serving:**
    - Fresh chimichurri sauce or pebre (a Chilean condiment made from tomatoes, onions, cilantro, and chili peppers)
    - Grilled vegetables (such as bell peppers, onions, and mushrooms)
    - Crusty bread

Instructions

1. **Prepare the Meat:**
    - If using a marinade, mix the olive oil, garlic, rosemary, red wine vinegar, soy sauce, paprika, cumin, salt, and pepper in a bowl.
    - Rub the marinade all over the beef ribs, sausages, and any other cuts of meat you're using. Let it marinate for at least 1 hour, or overnight for best results. If not marinating, simply season the meat with salt and pepper before grilling.
2. **Prepare the Grill:**
    - Preheat your grill to medium-high heat. If using a charcoal grill, let the coals burn until they are covered with a white ash.
    - If using a gas grill, preheat to medium-high.
3. **Grill the Meat:**
    - **Ribs and Steaks:** Place the beef ribs and any other steak cuts on the grill. Cook the ribs for about 4-5 minutes per side, or until they have a nice char and are cooked to your desired level of doneness. The flank or skirt steak usually takes 3-4 minutes per side for medium-rare.

- - **Sausages:** Grill the sausages for about 5-7 minutes, turning occasionally, until they are cooked through and have a crispy exterior.
  - **Optional Vegetables:** You can also grill vegetables alongside the meat. Brush them with olive oil and season with salt and pepper before grilling.
4. **Serve:**
   - **Rest the Meat:** Allow the grilled meat to rest for a few minutes before slicing.
   - **Serve with Condiments:** Serve the meat with fresh chimichurri sauce or pebre, and accompany it with grilled vegetables and crusty bread.

Tips:

- **Grill Temperature:** For a perfect Asado, maintain a consistent medium-high heat. Too high and the meat might burn; too low and it might not get a good sear.
- **Doneness:** Use a meat thermometer to ensure your steaks reach the desired doneness if needed (e.g., 130°F for medium-rare).

Asado is more than just a meal; it's a social gathering, so enjoy the process and share the food with family and friends!

Porotos Granados

Ingredients

- **For the Stew:**
    - 2 cups fresh or frozen cranberries or pinto beans (soaked overnight if dried)
    - 1 tbsp vegetable oil
    - 1 onion, chopped
    - 2 cloves garlic, minced
    - 1 red bell pepper, chopped
    - 1 cup corn kernels (fresh or frozen)
    - 1 medium tomato, chopped (or 1 cup canned diced tomatoes)
    - 1 medium zucchini, diced
    - 2 medium potatoes, peeled and diced
    - 1/2 cup fresh basil leaves, chopped (or 1 tbsp dried basil)
    - 1 tsp paprika
    - 1 tsp ground cumin
    - 1 bay leaf
    - 4 cups vegetable or chicken broth
    - Salt and pepper to taste
- **For Garnish:**
    - Fresh parsley or additional basil, chopped

Instructions

1. **Prepare the Beans:**
    - If using dried beans, soak them in water overnight. Drain and rinse before using.
    - If using fresh or frozen beans, skip the soaking step.
2. **Cook the Beans:**
    - In a large pot, cover the beans with water and bring to a boil. Reduce heat and simmer for about 30-40 minutes, or until the beans are tender. Drain and set aside.
3. **Prepare the Stew:**
    - Heat vegetable oil in a large pot or Dutch oven over medium heat.
    - Add chopped onion and minced garlic, cooking until softened and translucent.
    - Stir in the chopped red bell pepper and cook for another 5 minutes.
    - Add the corn kernels, chopped tomato, zucchini, and diced potatoes. Cook for another 5 minutes, stirring occasionally.
    - Add the cooked beans to the pot.
    - Stir in the chopped basil, paprika, cumin, bay leaf, salt, and pepper.
    - Pour in the vegetable or chicken broth and bring to a boil.
4. **Simmer the Stew:**

- Reduce heat to low and let the stew simmer for 20-30 minutes, or until the vegetables are tender and the flavors have melded together.
5. **Serve:**
   - Remove the bay leaf before serving.
   - Garnish with fresh parsley or additional basil if desired.
6. **Enjoy:**
   - Serve the Porotos Granados warm, ideally with a side of crusty bread or a fresh salad.

Tips:

- **Fresh Beans:** If using fresh beans, cook them until tender before adding them to the stew.
- **Seasoning:** Adjust seasoning to taste. Some variations of Porotos Granados include a touch of chili flakes for a bit of heat.
- **Vegetables:** You can also add other vegetables like carrots or green beans based on your preference.

Porotos Granados is a flavorful and satisfying dish that showcases the rich flavors of Chilean cuisine, perfect for a hearty lunch or dinner.

Pebre

Ingredients

- 1 cup fresh cilantro leaves, finely chopped
- 1/2 cup red onion, finely chopped
- 2 medium tomatoes, diced
- 1-2 cloves garlic, minced
- 1-2 jalapeños or green chilies, finely chopped (adjust to taste for heat)
- 2 tbsp olive oil
- 1-2 tbsp red wine vinegar or lime juice (adjust to taste)
- Salt and pepper to taste

Instructions

1. **Prepare the Ingredients:**
   - Finely chop the cilantro leaves, red onion, tomatoes, and jalapeños (or green chilies). Mince the garlic.
2. **Mix the Ingredients:**
   - In a bowl, combine the chopped cilantro, red onion, tomatoes, garlic, and jalapeños.
3. **Add Seasonings:**
   - Stir in the olive oil and red wine vinegar (or lime juice). Mix well.
4. **Season:**
   - Add salt and pepper to taste. Adjust seasoning as needed.
5. **Let It Rest:**
   - Allow the Pebre to sit for at least 30 minutes to let the flavors meld together. It can be served immediately, but it often tastes better after a little rest.
6. **Serve:**
   - Serve Pebre with bread, as a topping for meats, or alongside other Chilean dishes like empanadas or Pastel de Choclo.

Tips:

- **Heat Level:** Adjust the amount of jalapeño or green chili to control the heat level of your Pebre.
- **Acidity:** If you prefer a tangier flavor, you can add more red wine vinegar or lime juice.
- **Storage:** Pebre can be stored in the refrigerator for up to a week. The flavors may intensify over time.

Pebre is a versatile condiment that brings a burst of fresh, vibrant flavor to many dishes, making it a staple in Chilean cuisine.

Charquicán

Ingredients

- **For the Stew:**
    - 1 lb (450 g) beef stew meat or dried meat (charqui), soaked and shredded
    - 2 tbsp vegetable oil
    - 1 onion, chopped
    - 2 cloves garlic, minced
    - 2 medium potatoes, peeled and diced
    - 1 cup butternut squash or pumpkin, peeled and diced
    - 2 carrots, peeled and diced
    - 1 cup green beans, chopped
    - 1 cup corn kernels (fresh, frozen, or canned)
    - 1-2 tsp paprika
    - 1 tsp ground cumin
    - 1 bay leaf
    - 4 cups beef or vegetable broth
    - Salt and pepper to taste
- **For Garnish (Optional):**
    - Fresh parsley, chopped

Instructions

1. **Prepare the Meat:**
    - If using dried meat (charqui), soak it in water for several hours or overnight to rehydrate and remove excess salt. Shred the meat after soaking. If using fresh beef stew meat, you can skip this step.
2. **Cook the Meat:**
    - Heat vegetable oil in a large pot or Dutch oven over medium heat.
    - Add the chopped onion and garlic, cooking until softened and translucent.
    - Add the meat and cook until browned.
3. **Prepare the Stew:**
    - Add the diced potatoes, butternut squash (or pumpkin), carrots, green beans, and corn to the pot.
    - Stir in the paprika, cumin, and bay leaf.
    - Pour in the beef or vegetable broth and bring to a boil.
    - Reduce heat to low, cover, and simmer for about 30-40 minutes, or until the vegetables are tender and the meat is cooked through.
4. **Adjust Seasoning:**
    - Season with salt and pepper to taste. Remove the bay leaf before serving.
5. **Serve:**

- Ladle the Charquicán into bowls and garnish with fresh parsley if desired.
- Serve warm with crusty bread or a side salad.

Tips:

- **Meat Choices:** If you prefer not to use dried meat, you can substitute with fresh beef or even chicken.
- **Vegetables:** Feel free to adjust the vegetables based on your preferences or what you have on hand.
- **Consistency:** If the stew is too thick, you can add a bit more broth or water to reach your desired consistency.

Charquicán is a versatile and hearty dish that brings together a delightful mix of flavors and textures, making it a beloved choice in Chilean cuisine.

Pastel de Jaiba

Ingredients

- **For the Filling:**
    - 1 lb (450 g) fresh or canned crab meat, drained
    - 2 tbsp butter
    - 1 onion, finely chopped
    - 2 cloves garlic, minced
    - 1/2 cup white wine or chicken broth
    - 1 cup heavy cream
    - 1/2 cup mayonnaise
    - 2 large eggs
    - 1/4 cup fresh parsley, chopped
    - 1/4 cup fresh cilantro, chopped (optional)
    - 1/2 tsp paprika
    - 1/2 tsp ground cumin
    - Salt and pepper to taste
- **For the Topping:**
    - 1/2 cup breadcrumbs
    - 2 tbsp grated Parmesan cheese
    - 2 tbsp melted butter
- **For the Crust (Optional):**
    - Pre-made pie crust or puff pastry (if using a crust)

Instructions

1. **Prepare the Filling:**
    - In a large skillet, melt the butter over medium heat.
    - Add the chopped onion and garlic, cooking until softened and translucent.
    - Pour in the white wine or chicken broth and cook for a few minutes, allowing it to reduce slightly.
    - Stir in the heavy cream and bring to a gentle simmer.
    - In a bowl, combine the mayonnaise, eggs, parsley, cilantro (if using), paprika, cumin, salt, and pepper. Mix well.
    - Gently fold in the crab meat.
    - Pour the crab mixture into the skillet and stir to combine. Cook for an additional 5 minutes, then remove from heat.
2. **Prepare the Crust (if using):**
    - Preheat your oven to 375°F (190°C).
    - If using a pie crust or puff pastry, fit it into a pie dish or baking dish. Trim any excess dough.

3. **Assemble the Pastel de Jaiba:**
   - Pour the crab filling into the prepared crust, spreading it evenly.
4. **Prepare the Topping:**
   - In a small bowl, mix the breadcrumbs with the grated Parmesan cheese and melted butter.
   - Sprinkle the breadcrumb mixture evenly over the top of the crab filling.
5. **Bake:**
   - Place the baking dish in the preheated oven.
   - Bake for 25-30 minutes, or until the top is golden brown and the filling is set and bubbly.
6. **Serve:**
   - Let the Pastel de Jaiba cool slightly before serving.
   - Garnish with additional chopped parsley if desired.

Tips:

- **Crab Meat:** If using canned crab meat, make sure to drain it well and pick out any shell pieces.
- **Creaminess:** For extra creaminess, you can substitute some of the heavy cream with cream cheese or sour cream.
- **Crust:** If you prefer not to use a crust, you can bake the filling as a crustless pie or use a simple buttered breadcrumb topping.

Pastel de Jaiba is a rich and indulgent dish that showcases the delicate flavors of crab, making it a special treat for any occasion.

Ensalada Chilena

Ingredients

- 4 ripe tomatoes, diced
- 1 red onion, thinly sliced
- 1/2 cup fresh cilantro, chopped
- 2-3 tbsp olive oil
- 1-2 tbsp red wine vinegar or lemon juice
- Salt and pepper to taste

Instructions

1. **Prepare the Vegetables:**
   - Dice the tomatoes into bite-sized pieces.
   - Thinly slice the red onion. To reduce the pungency of the onion, you can soak the slices in cold water for about 10 minutes, then drain and pat dry.
2. **Mix the Salad:**
   - In a large bowl, combine the diced tomatoes, sliced onion, and chopped cilantro.
3. **Dress the Salad:**
   - Drizzle the olive oil and red wine vinegar (or lemon juice) over the salad.
   - Toss gently to combine and coat the vegetables evenly.
4. **Season:**
   - Add salt and pepper to taste.
   - Toss again to mix the seasonings.
5. **Serve:**
   - Let the salad sit for about 10-15 minutes before serving to allow the flavors to meld.
   - Serve fresh as a side dish with your favorite Chilean dishes or any meal.

Tips:

- **Variations:** Some variations include adding sliced avocado or cucumber for extra texture.
- **Herbs:** If you prefer, you can substitute cilantro with fresh parsley for a different flavor profile.
- **Onion:** If you want a milder onion flavor, you can use white or yellow onions instead of red.

Ensalada Chilena is a refreshing and easy-to-make salad that captures the essence of Chilean cuisine with its straightforward ingredients and vibrant flavors.

Caldillo de Congrio

Ingredients

- **For the Stew:**
    - 2 lbs (900 g) conger eel or another firm white fish (like cod or haddock), cut into chunks
    - 2 tbsp vegetable oil
    - 1 onion, chopped
    - 2 cloves garlic, minced
    - 2 carrots, peeled and sliced
    - 2 medium potatoes, peeled and diced
    - 1 cup butternut squash or pumpkin, peeled and diced
    - 1/2 cup green beans, chopped
    - 1/2 cup corn kernels (fresh, frozen, or canned)
    - 1 cup diced tomatoes (fresh or canned)
    - 4 cups fish or vegetable broth
    - 1 bay leaf
    - 1 tsp paprika
    - 1 tsp dried oregano
    - 1/2 tsp ground cumin
    - 1/2 tsp ground black pepper
    - Salt to taste
    - 1/4 cup fresh parsley or cilantro, chopped (for garnish)

Instructions

1. **Prepare the Fish:**
    - If using fresh conger eel, clean and cut it into chunks. If using frozen, thaw and cut it into pieces. Season the fish with a bit of salt and pepper.
2. **Cook the Vegetables:**
    - Heat vegetable oil in a large pot or Dutch oven over medium heat.
    - Add the chopped onion and garlic, cooking until softened and translucent.
3. **Add the Broth and Vegetables:**
    - Stir in the carrots, potatoes, butternut squash (or pumpkin), and green beans.
    - Add the diced tomatoes and cook for a few minutes.
    - Pour in the fish or vegetable broth and bring to a boil.
4. **Season the Stew:**
    - Add the bay leaf, paprika, oregano, cumin, black pepper, and salt.
    - Reduce heat to low and simmer for about 20-25 minutes, or until the vegetables are tender.
5. **Add the Fish:**

- Gently add the fish chunks to the pot.
- Simmer for an additional 10-15 minutes, or until the fish is cooked through and flakes easily with a fork.

6. **Serve:**
   - Remove the bay leaf before serving.
   - Garnish with fresh parsley or cilantro.
   - Serve the Caldillo de Congrio hot, ideally with crusty bread or a side of rice.

Tips:

- **Fish:** If you can't find conger eel, you can substitute with another firm white fish. Adjust cooking time based on the thickness of the fish pieces.
- **Vegetables:** Feel free to add or substitute other vegetables based on your preference or availability.
- **Broth:** Using homemade fish broth or a high-quality store-bought broth will enhance the flavor of the stew.

Caldillo de Congrio is a beloved dish in Chile, celebrated for its rich and satisfying flavors. Enjoy this classic Chilean stew as a comforting meal on a cool day or as a special treat for family and friends.

Sopaipillas

Ingredients:

- 2 1/2 cups all-purpose flour
- 1/2 teaspoon salt
- 1 tablespoon baking powder
- 1/4 cup lard, shortening, or unsalted butter
- 1 cup warm water (approximately)
- Oil for frying (vegetable or canola oil works well)

Instructions:

1. **Prepare the Dough:**
   - In a large bowl, whisk together the flour, salt, and baking powder.
   - Cut in the lard (or shortening/butter) until the mixture resembles coarse crumbs.
   - Gradually add warm water, mixing until a soft dough forms. You might not need all the water, so add it slowly.
   - Knead the dough on a lightly floured surface until smooth, about 2-3 minutes.
2. **Roll and Cut:**
   - Roll out the dough to about 1/8-inch thickness.
   - Cut the dough into squares or rectangles (about 2-3 inches).
3. **Heat the Oil:**
   - Heat about 2 inches of oil in a deep skillet or frying pan over medium-high heat until it reaches 375°F (190°C). You can test the oil by dropping a small piece of dough into it; if it floats and bubbles, it's ready.
4. **Fry the Sopaipillas:**
   - Carefully place the dough pieces into the hot oil, a few at a time, without overcrowding the pan.
   - Fry until they puff up and turn golden brown, about 1-2 minutes per side.
   - Remove with a slotted spoon and drain on paper towels.
5. **Serve:**
   - While still warm, dust with powdered sugar or drizzle with honey if desired. You can also serve them with savory dishes if you prefer.

Enjoy your homemade sopaipillas! They're perfect for a cozy treat or as a fun addition to any meal.

Humitas

Ingredients:

- 4 cups fresh corn kernels (about 6-8 ears of corn)
- 1 cup finely chopped onion
- 2 tablespoons butter or oil
- 1/2 cup crumbled queso fresco or cotija cheese (optional)
- 1/4 cup fresh basil or cilantro leaves, chopped
- 1 teaspoon baking powder
- Salt and pepper to taste
- Corn husks (soaked in warm water for about 30 minutes, then drained)

Instructions:

1. **Prepare the Corn:**
   - Remove the kernels from the cobs. Use a food processor or blender to pulse the corn kernels until you have a smooth, creamy mixture. You can also use a grater if you prefer a more rustic texture.
2. **Cook the Onion:**
   - In a skillet, heat the butter or oil over medium heat. Add the chopped onion and cook until softened and translucent, about 5 minutes. Allow to cool slightly.
3. **Mix the Dough:**
   - In a large bowl, combine the corn mixture, cooked onion, baking powder, chopped basil or cilantro, and cheese (if using). Season with salt and pepper to taste.
4. **Assemble the Humitas:**
   - Take a soaked corn husk and place about 2-3 tablespoons of the corn mixture in the center. Fold the sides of the husk over the mixture and then fold the bottom up to form a packet. Secure with a piece of string or a strip of husk if needed.
5. **Steam the Humitas:**
   - Place the wrapped humitas in a large steamer basket or a large pot with a steaming rack. Steam over boiling water for about 45-60 minutes, or until the corn mixture is set and cooked through. You might need to check and add water to the pot as needed during steaming.
6. **Serve:**
   - Allow the humitas to cool slightly before unwrapping. Serve warm as a side dish or a main course. They're often enjoyed with a dollop of sour cream or a spicy salsa on the side.

Humitas are versatile and can be adapted to suit different tastes, including adding ingredients like spices, meats, or vegetables. They're a comforting and flavorful dish perfect for a variety of occasions!

Paila Marina

Ingredients:

- 1/4 cup olive oil
- 1 large onion, finely chopped
- 4 garlic cloves, minced
- 1 large tomato, chopped
- 1 cup white wine (optional, but adds great flavor)
- 4 cups seafood or fish stock (you can use water if you don't have stock)
- 1 cup water (if needed to adjust consistency)
- 1 bay leaf
- 1 teaspoon paprika
- 1/2 teaspoon ground cumin
- Salt and black pepper to taste
- 1/2 teaspoon dried oregano
- 1 lb (450g) firm white fish (such as cod, halibut, or sea bass), cut into chunks
- 1/2 lb (225g) shrimp, peeled and deveined
- 1/2 lb (225g) mussels or clams, cleaned
- 1/2 lb (225g) squid, cleaned and cut into rings
- 1/2 cup chopped fresh parsley
- Juice of 1 lemon
- Crusty bread for serving

Instructions:

1. **Prepare the Base:**
    - Heat the olive oil in a large pot or Dutch oven over medium heat. Add the chopped onion and cook until softened, about 5 minutes.
    - Add the minced garlic and cook for an additional minute until fragrant.
    - Stir in the chopped tomato and cook until it breaks down and the mixture starts to thicken, about 5 minutes.
2. **Add Liquids and Seasonings:**
    - Pour in the white wine (if using) and cook for a couple of minutes until it has reduced slightly.
    - Add the seafood or fish stock and water. Stir in the bay leaf, paprika, cumin, salt, pepper, and dried oregano.
    - Bring the mixture to a boil, then reduce the heat and let it simmer for about 10 minutes to allow the flavors to meld.
3. **Cook the Seafood:**
    - Add the fish chunks and simmer for about 5 minutes.

- Add the shrimp, mussels (or clams), and squid. Continue to simmer until the seafood is cooked through and the mussels or clams have opened, about 5-7 minutes. Discard any mussels or clams that do not open.
4. **Finish the Dish:**
    - Stir in the chopped parsley and lemon juice. Adjust the seasoning with more salt and pepper if needed.
5. **Serve:**
    - Ladle the paila marina into bowls and serve with crusty bread on the side for dipping.

Paila Marina is a delightful and satisfying dish, full of fresh seafood flavors and aromatic spices. It's perfect for sharing with family and friends, and the rich broth is great for soaking up with good bread. Enjoy!

Carbonada

Ingredients:

- 2 tablespoons olive oil
- 1 lb (450g) beef stew meat (cut into cubes)
- 1 large onion, chopped
- 3 garlic cloves, minced
- 1 large carrot, peeled and chopped
- 1 large potato, peeled and chopped
- 1 cup butternut squash or pumpkin, peeled and chopped
- 1 cup corn kernels (fresh, frozen, or canned)
- 1/2 cup green beans, cut into pieces
- 1 cup cooked rice (optional, for added heartiness)
- 4 cups beef or vegetable broth
- 1 cup canned tomatoes (diced or crushed)
- 1 tablespoon paprika
- 1 teaspoon dried oregano
- 1 teaspoon ground cumin
- Salt and black pepper to taste
- 1/2 cup dried apricots (optional, for a hint of sweetness)
- Fresh parsley (chopped, for garnish)

Instructions:

1. **Brown the Meat:**
    - Heat the olive oil in a large pot or Dutch oven over medium-high heat. Add the beef cubes and cook until browned on all sides. Remove the meat from the pot and set aside.
2. **Sauté the Vegetables:**
    - In the same pot, add the chopped onion and cook until softened and translucent, about 5 minutes. Add the minced garlic and cook for another minute.
3. **Add the Vegetables and Spices:**
    - Add the chopped carrot, potato, and butternut squash or pumpkin to the pot. Stir in the paprika, dried oregano, and ground cumin. Cook for about 5 minutes, allowing the spices to toast slightly.
4. **Combine Ingredients:**
    - Return the browned meat to the pot. Pour in the beef or vegetable broth and diced tomatoes. Bring to a boil, then reduce the heat to low. Simmer for about 30-40 minutes, or until the meat and vegetables are tender.
5. **Add Remaining Ingredients:**
    - Stir in the corn kernels, green beans, and dried apricots (if using). Continue to cook for another 10-15 minutes until all the vegetables are tender and the flavors

are well combined. If you're using cooked rice, stir it in during the last few minutes of cooking to warm through.
6. **Season and Serve:**
    - Adjust the seasoning with salt and pepper to taste. Garnish with chopped fresh parsley.
7. **Enjoy:**
    - Serve the carbonada hot, ideally with crusty bread on the side.

Carbonada is a versatile dish that can be adapted based on the ingredients you have on hand or your personal preferences. The inclusion of dried fruit is a unique touch that gives the stew a distinctive flavor, but you can omit it if you prefer a more savory version. Enjoy this comforting and flavorful Chilean classic!

Pan Amasado

Ingredients:

- 4 cups all-purpose flour
- 1 tablespoon baking powder
- 1 teaspoon salt
- 1/2 cup lard, shortening, or unsalted butter
- 1 1/2 cups warm water (adjust as needed)
- 1 tablespoon sugar (optional, for a slightly sweeter bread)
- 1 tablespoon olive oil (optional, for added flavor)

Instructions:

1. **Prepare the Dough:**
   - In a large bowl, whisk together the flour, baking powder, and salt. If you're using sugar, add it here as well.
   - Cut in the lard (or shortening/butter) until the mixture resembles coarse crumbs.
   - Gradually add the warm water, mixing until a soft dough forms. You might not need all the water, so add it slowly.
   - Knead the dough on a lightly floured surface until smooth and elastic, about 5-7 minutes.
2. **Shape the Bread:**
   - Preheat your oven to 375°F (190°C).
   - Divide the dough into 8-10 equal portions and shape each portion into a round or slightly flattened loaf, about 1 inch thick.
   - Place the shaped dough on a baking sheet lined with parchment paper or lightly greased.
3. **Optional Glaze:**
   - For a slightly crispier crust, you can brush the tops of the dough with a little olive oil before baking.
4. **Bake:**
   - Bake in the preheated oven for 20-25 minutes, or until the bread is golden brown and sounds hollow when tapped on the bottom.
   - Remove from the oven and let cool slightly on a wire rack before serving.

Tips:

- **Flour Adjustment:** Depending on the type of flour and humidity, you might need to adjust the amount of water slightly. The dough should be soft but not sticky.
- **Serving:** Pan amasado is versatile. You can enjoy it plain, with butter, or with your favorite cheese or cold cuts. It's also great for making sandwiches.

Pan Amasado is a wonderful bread to bake at home, offering a comforting, rustic flavor that's perfect for any meal. Enjoy the process of making it and the delicious results!

Mote con Huesillos

Ingredients:

- 1 cup dried peaches (huesillos)
- 1 cup wheat kernels (mote), soaked overnight or for at least 8 hours
- 1/2 cup sugar (or to taste)
- 1-2 cinnamon sticks
- 1 teaspoon vanilla extract (optional)
- 1-2 cloves (optional)
- Water
- Ice cubes (for serving)
- Fresh mint (for garnish, optional)

Instructions:

1. **Prepare the Wheat:**
   - Drain the soaked wheat and rinse it well.
   - In a large pot, cover the wheat with fresh water. Bring to a boil, then reduce the heat and simmer for about 30-45 minutes, or until the wheat is tender but still has a slight chew. Drain and set aside.
2. **Prepare the Peaches:**
   - In another pot, place the dried peaches and cover them with water. Add the cinnamon sticks, cloves (if using), and sugar.
   - Bring to a boil, then reduce the heat and simmer for about 30 minutes, or until the peaches are softened and the liquid has thickened slightly into a syrup.
3. **Combine Ingredients:**
   - Once the peaches are softened, add the cooked wheat to the pot with the peaches. Stir well to combine and heat through.
   - Remove from heat and stir in the vanilla extract, if using.
4. **Cool and Serve:**
   - Let the mixture cool to room temperature. It can be served either chilled or at room temperature.
   - To serve, place some of the peach pieces and wheat in a glass or bowl, then pour the liquid over it. Add ice cubes if you prefer it chilled.
5. **Garnish (Optional):**
   - Garnish with fresh mint if desired.

Mote con Huesillos is a delightful and traditional Chilean treat that's perfect for enjoying on a warm day or as a special treat. It's both a drink and a dessert in one, offering a unique combination of flavors and textures. Enjoy!

Chacarero

Ingredients:

- 1 lb (450g) beef steak (such as sirloin or flank steak)
- Salt and black pepper to taste
- 1 tablespoon vegetable oil (for grilling)
- 4 sandwich rolls (or Italian rolls, preferably crusty)
- 1 cup green beans, trimmed and cut into small pieces
- 2-3 ripe tomatoes, sliced
- 1/2 cup mayonnaise
- 1-2 tablespoons ají verde (Chile's spicy green sauce) or a similar hot sauce
- Optional: lettuce leaves for added crunch

For the Ají Verde (Green Sauce):

- 1/2 cup fresh cilantro
- 1-2 green chilies (mild or hot, depending on your preference)
- 2-3 garlic cloves
- 1 tablespoon olive oil
- 1 tablespoon lemon juice
- Salt to taste

Instructions:

1. **Prepare the Ají Verde (Green Sauce):**
    - In a blender or food processor, combine the cilantro, green chilies, garlic, olive oil, and lemon juice.
    - Blend until smooth. Adjust seasoning with salt to taste. Set aside.
2. **Cook the Beef:**
    - Season the beef steak with salt and pepper.
    - Heat the vegetable oil in a skillet or on a grill over medium-high heat.
    - Cook the steak for about 3-5 minutes per side, or until it reaches your desired level of doneness (medium-rare to medium is common).
    - Remove from heat and let it rest for a few minutes before slicing it thinly against the grain.
3. **Prepare the Green Beans:**
    - Bring a small pot of water to a boil.
    - Add the green beans and blanch for about 2-3 minutes, or until they are bright green and tender-crisp.
    - Drain and immediately transfer the beans to a bowl of ice water to stop the cooking process. Drain again.
4. **Assemble the Sandwich:**

- Slice the rolls in half and lightly toast them if desired.
- Spread a layer of mayonnaise on the bottom half of each roll.
- Top with slices of beef, then add a layer of green beans, tomato slices, and optional lettuce.
- Drizzle with ají verde to taste.

5. **Serve:**
   - Place the top half of the roll on the sandwich and serve immediately.

Chacarero is a delicious and satisfying sandwich with a unique combination of ingredients. The spicy ají verde adds a distinctive kick, and the fresh vegetables and tender beef make it a flavorful meal. Enjoy this classic Chilean treat!

Confit de Pato

Ingredients:

- 4 duck legs (with thighs)
- 2 tablespoons kosher salt
- 1 tablespoon coarse black pepper
- 4 cloves garlic, minced
- 1 tablespoon fresh thyme leaves (or 1 teaspoon dried thyme)
- 1 teaspoon dried rosemary (or 1 tablespoon fresh rosemary, chopped)
- 2 bay leaves
- 2 cups duck fat (or enough to fully submerge the duck legs; you can substitute with a mixture of vegetable oil and a bit of butter if duck fat is unavailable)

Instructions:

1. **Prepare the Duck Legs:**
    - Pat the duck legs dry with paper towels.
    - Rub the duck legs all over with kosher salt, black pepper, minced garlic, thyme, rosemary, and bay leaves.
    - Place the seasoned duck legs in a dish, cover, and refrigerate for at least 12 hours, or up to 24 hours. This process is called curing and helps to flavor the meat.
2. **Rinse and Dry:**
    - After curing, remove the duck legs from the refrigerator.
    - Rinse off the seasoning under cold water and pat the duck legs dry with paper towels.
3. **Cook the Duck Legs:**
    - Preheat your oven to 275°F (135°C).
    - In a large ovenproof pot or Dutch oven, melt the duck fat over low heat.
    - Add the duck legs to the pot, making sure they are fully submerged in the fat. If you don't have enough fat, you can top it off with a bit of vegetable oil.
    - Cover the pot with a lid or aluminum foil and place it in the preheated oven.
    - Cook slowly for about 2.5 to 3 hours, or until the duck meat is very tender and easily pulls away from the bone.
4. **Crisp the Duck Legs:**
    - Once the duck legs are cooked, remove them from the fat and set them on a plate lined with paper towels to drain.
    - Heat a skillet over medium-high heat. Add a small amount of duck fat to the pan.
    - Place the duck legs skin-side down in the hot skillet. Cook for about 5-7 minutes, or until the skin is crispy and golden brown.

- Flip the legs and cook for an additional 1-2 minutes to crisp the other side if desired.
5. **Serve:**
    - Serve the confit de pato hot, typically with sides like roasted potatoes, braised greens, or a simple salad. It pairs wonderfully with a glass of red wine or a crisp white.

Tips:

- **Storage:** Duck confit can be stored in the fat in the refrigerator for several weeks. Make sure the meat is fully submerged in fat to preserve it.
- **Using Leftover Fat:** The leftover duck fat can be strained and stored in the refrigerator for future use. It's excellent for cooking potatoes or other vegetables.

Confit de Pato is a luxurious and flavorful dish that's perfect for special occasions or a comforting meal at home. Enjoy the crispy skin and tender meat of this classic French preparation!

Chile en Nogada

Ingredients:

For the Chiles:

- 6-8 large poblano peppers
- 2 tablespoons vegetable oil

For the Picadillo Filling:

- 1 lb (450g) ground pork (or a mix of pork and beef)
- 1 large onion, finely chopped
- 2 garlic cloves, minced
- 1 large tomato, chopped
- 1/2 cup almonds, chopped
- 1/2 cup raisins
- 1/2 cup candied fruit (such as citron or orange peel, chopped)
- 1/2 cup fresh or canned peaches, chopped
- 1/2 cup fresh or canned apple, chopped
- 1/4 cup pine nuts (optional)
- 1/4 teaspoon ground cinnamon
- 1/4 teaspoon ground cloves
- 1/4 teaspoon allspice
- 1/4 cup white wine (optional)
- Salt and black pepper to taste

For the Nogada Sauce:

- 1 cup walnuts, shelled and soaked in milk for at least 2 hours
- 1/2 cup milk (for soaking walnuts)
- 1/4 cup sugar (adjust to taste)
- 1/4 teaspoon ground cinnamon
- 1 tablespoon sherry or brandy (optional)
- Salt to taste

For Garnish:

- 1/2 cup pomegranate seeds
- Fresh parsley, chopped (for garnish)

Instructions:

1. **Prepare the Chiles:**

- Roast the poblano peppers over an open flame or under the broiler, turning frequently, until the skin is blackened and blistered.
- Place the roasted peppers in a plastic bag or covered bowl to steam for about 15 minutes. This will make peeling easier.
- Peel the skins off the peppers, then carefully make a slit along one side of each pepper and remove the seeds and membranes. Set aside.

2. **Prepare the Picadillo Filling:**
   - In a large skillet, heat the vegetable oil over medium heat. Add the chopped onion and cook until softened.
   - Add the garlic and cook for another minute.
   - Add the ground pork (and beef if using) and cook until browned, breaking up the meat with a spoon.
   - Stir in the chopped tomato and cook for a few minutes until it starts to break down.
   - Add the almonds, raisins, candied fruit, peaches, apple, and pine nuts (if using). Mix well.
   - Add the cinnamon, cloves, and allspice. If using, pour in the white wine.
   - Simmer for 10-15 minutes until the mixture is thickened and the flavors are well combined. Season with salt and pepper to taste. Allow to cool slightly.

3. **Prepare the Nogada Sauce:**
   - Drain the walnuts and place them in a blender or food processor. Add the milk, sugar, and cinnamon.
   - Blend until smooth. You can adjust the thickness by adding more milk if needed.
   - Stir in the sherry or brandy if using, and season with salt to taste.

4. **Assemble the Dish:**
   - Stuff each roasted poblano pepper with the picadillo filling.
   - Place the stuffed peppers in a serving dish.
   - Pour the nogada sauce over the stuffed peppers.

5. **Garnish and Serve:**
   - Sprinkle pomegranate seeds over the top and garnish with chopped fresh parsley.
   - Serve at room temperature or slightly chilled.

Chile en Nogada is a festive and flavorful dish that embodies the essence of Mexican cuisine. The combination of sweet and savory elements, along with the creamy walnut sauce and pomegranate seeds, makes it a truly special and delicious dish. Enjoy!

Arroz con Mariscos

Ingredients:

- 2 tablespoons olive oil
- 1 onion, finely chopped
- 3 garlic cloves, minced
- 1 red bell pepper, chopped
- 1 green bell pepper, chopped
- 2 large tomatoes, chopped (or 1 cup canned tomatoes, diced)
- 1 teaspoon paprika
- 1 teaspoon ground cumin
- 1 teaspoon dried oregano
- 1/2 teaspoon ground turmeric (for color)
- 1 cup Arborio or short-grain rice
- 1/2 cup white wine (optional)
- 2 cups seafood or chicken broth
- 1/2 cup frozen peas
- 1/2 cup chopped fresh cilantro (plus more for garnish)
- 1 lb (450g) mixed seafood (such as shrimp, squid, mussels, clams, and fish), cleaned and cut into bite-sized pieces
- 1 lemon, cut into wedges (for serving)
- Salt and black pepper to taste

Instructions:

1. **Prepare the Base:**
   - Heat the olive oil in a large, deep skillet or Dutch oven over medium heat.
   - Add the chopped onion and cook until softened and translucent, about 5 minutes.
   - Stir in the minced garlic, red and green bell peppers, and cook for another 2-3 minutes until the peppers are tender.
2. **Add Tomatoes and Spices:**
   - Add the chopped tomatoes, paprika, cumin, oregano, and turmeric. Cook for about 5 minutes, until the tomatoes break down and the mixture becomes fragrant.
3. **Cook the Rice:**
   - Stir in the rice, coating it well with the tomato mixture.
   - Pour in the white wine, if using, and let it simmer for a few minutes until it has mostly evaporated.
   - Add the seafood or chicken broth and bring to a boil.
   - Reduce the heat to low, cover, and let it simmer for about 15-20 minutes, or until the rice is almost cooked and has absorbed most of the liquid.

4. **Add Seafood:**
   - Gently stir in the mixed seafood and frozen peas.
   - Continue to cook, covered, for another 5-7 minutes, or until the seafood is cooked through and the rice is tender. If the mixture seems dry, add a bit more broth or water as needed.
5. **Finish and Serve:**
   - Stir in the chopped fresh cilantro and adjust seasoning with salt and black pepper to taste.
   - Garnish with additional cilantro and serve with lemon wedges on the side.

Tips:

- **Seafood Selection:** You can use any combination of seafood you prefer or have on hand. Ensure that all seafood is prepped and cleaned before adding it to the dish.
- **Rice:** Short-grain rice is preferred for its ability to absorb flavors well. Arborio rice works well, but you can use other types if needed.
- **Broth:** If you don't have seafood broth, chicken broth works as a substitute.

Arroz con Mariscos is a versatile dish that can be adjusted to suit your taste preferences and the seafood available to you. It's a flavorful, satisfying meal perfect for special occasions or a delightful weeknight dinner. Enjoy!

Merluza a la Plancha

Ingredients:

- 4 hake fillets (or other firm white fish like cod or haddock), skin-on or skinless
- 2 tablespoons olive oil
- 2 garlic cloves, minced
- 1 teaspoon smoked paprika (or regular paprika)
- 1 lemon, cut into wedges
- Salt and black pepper to taste
- Fresh parsley (chopped, for garnish)

Instructions:

1. **Prepare the Fish:**
    - Pat the hake fillets dry with paper towels to ensure a good sear.
    - Season the fillets with salt, black pepper, and smoked paprika on both sides.
2. **Heat the Pan:**
    - Heat olive oil in a large skillet or griddle over medium-high heat. Ensure the pan is hot before adding the fish to get a good sear.
3. **Cook the Fish:**
    - Add the minced garlic to the pan and cook for about 30 seconds, or until fragrant. Be careful not to let the garlic burn.
    - Place the hake fillets in the pan, skin-side down if the skin is on. Cook for about 3-4 minutes on each side, or until the fish is golden brown and cooked through. The cooking time may vary depending on the thickness of the fillets.
4. **Serve:**
    - Remove the fish from the pan and place it on a serving plate.
    - Garnish with chopped fresh parsley and serve with lemon wedges on the side.

Tips:

- **Freshness:** Use fresh hake or other white fish for the best flavor. If using frozen fish, make sure it is thoroughly thawed and patted dry before cooking.
- **Pan:** Use a non-stick or well-seasoned cast iron skillet to prevent the fish from sticking.
- **Variations:** You can add a squeeze of lemon juice over the fish just before serving or drizzle with a bit more olive oil for added richness.

Merluza a la Plancha is a straightforward and elegant dish that highlights the delicate taste of the fish. It's perfect for a quick weeknight dinner or a light, healthy meal. Enjoy with a side of vegetables or a fresh salad for a complete meal!

Tortilla de Papas

Ingredients:

- 4 large potatoes (about 1 lb or 450g)
- 1 large onion (optional, but recommended for flavor)
- 6 large eggs
- 1/4 cup olive oil (for cooking the potatoes and onions)
- Salt and black pepper to taste

Instructions:

1. **Prepare the Potatoes:**
   - Peel the potatoes and slice them thinly, about 1/8 inch (3 mm) thick. If you prefer, you can cut them into small cubes.
   - Optionally, you can soak the sliced potatoes in cold water for about 30 minutes to remove excess starch, then drain and pat them dry.
2. **Cook the Potatoes and Onion:**
   - Heat the olive oil in a large non-stick skillet or frying pan over medium heat.
   - Add the sliced potatoes (and onions if using) to the pan. Season with salt and cook, stirring occasionally, until the potatoes are tender and lightly golden, about 20-25 minutes.
   - Remove the potatoes and onions from the pan using a slotted spoon and drain them on paper towels to remove excess oil.
3. **Prepare the Egg Mixture:**
   - In a large bowl, beat the eggs and season with a bit of salt and black pepper.
   - Gently fold in the cooked potatoes and onions until well combined.
4. **Cook the Tortilla:**
   - Wipe out the skillet and add a little more olive oil. Heat the pan over medium heat.
   - Pour the potato and egg mixture into the pan, spreading it out evenly. Cook for about 5-7 minutes, or until the edges start to set and the bottom is golden brown.
   - To flip the tortilla, place a large plate over the pan and carefully invert the tortilla onto the plate. Add a bit more oil to the pan if necessary and slide the tortilla back into the pan to cook the other side.
   - Cook for another 5-7 minutes, or until the tortilla is set in the middle and the bottom is golden brown.
5. **Serve:**
   - Slide the tortilla onto a serving plate and let it cool slightly before slicing. It can be served warm, at room temperature, or cold.

Tips:

- **Cooking Time:** Adjust the cooking time based on the thickness of the tortilla and your preference for doneness. It should be slightly moist in the center but fully cooked.
- **Flipping:** If you're nervous about flipping the tortilla, you can use a second plate to help flip it, or you can cook it fully on one side and then place it under a broiler to finish cooking the top.
- **Variations:** Feel free to add ingredients like bell peppers, chorizo, or herbs to the potato and egg mixture for additional flavor.

Tortilla de Papas is a beloved Spanish dish that's both hearty and comforting. It's perfect for a quick meal or a centerpiece for a tapas-style spread. Enjoy!

Chorillana

Ingredients:

For the Fries:

- 4 large potatoes, peeled
- Vegetable oil, for frying
- Salt, to taste

For the Beef Topping:

- 1 lb (450g) sirloin steak or other tender beef cuts, thinly sliced
- 2 tablespoons vegetable oil
- 1 large onion, thinly sliced
- 2 garlic cloves, minced
- 1 teaspoon paprika
- 1 teaspoon ground cumin
- Salt and black pepper, to taste

For Garnish:

- **4 large eggs**
- **Chopped fresh parsley** (for garnish, optional)

Instructions:

1. **Prepare the Fries:**
    - Peel the potatoes and cut them into thin strips for fries.
    - Rinse the potato strips in cold water and then pat them dry with paper towels.
    - Heat the vegetable oil in a deep fryer or large heavy-bottomed pot to 350°F (175°C).
    - Fry the potato strips in batches until they are golden brown and crispy, about 3-5 minutes per batch.
    - Remove the fries with a slotted spoon and drain them on paper towels. Season with salt immediately.
2. **Cook the Beef Topping:**
    - Heat vegetable oil in a large skillet over medium-high heat.
    - Add the thinly sliced onions and cook until they start to soften and become translucent, about 5 minutes.
    - Add the minced garlic and cook for another minute.
    - Add the beef slices to the skillet and cook until browned and cooked through, about 5-7 minutes.

- Season with paprika, cumin, salt, and black pepper. Mix well and cook for another minute or so to allow the flavors to meld together.
3. **Cook the Eggs:**
    - While the beef is cooking, heat a small non-stick skillet over medium heat.
    - Fry the eggs to your liking (sunny-side up or over-easy is common).
4. **Assemble the Chorillana:**
    - Arrange the hot fries on a large serving plate or dish.
    - Top the fries with the beef and onion mixture.
    - Place the fried eggs on top of the beef mixture.
    - Garnish with chopped fresh parsley if desired.
5. **Serve:**
    - Serve the Chorillana immediately while the fries are crispy and the eggs are still warm.

Tips:

- **Beef:** Thinly slicing the beef helps it cook quickly and evenly. You can also use other cuts of beef if you prefer.
- **Frying:** Ensure the oil is hot enough before adding the fries to achieve a crispy texture. Don't overcrowd the pot or fryer.
- **Eggs:** You can cook the eggs to your preference, but sunny-side up or over-easy is typical for Chorillana.

Chorillana is a delicious and indulgent dish perfect for sharing with friends or family. Its combination of crispy fries, savory beef, and runny eggs makes it a comfort food classic. Enjoy!

Tarta de Mariscos

Ingredients:

For the Pastry Crust:

- 1 1/2 cups all-purpose flour
- 1/2 cup unsalted butter, cold and cut into small pieces
- 1/4 teaspoon salt
- 1/4 cup ice water (more if needed)

For the Seafood Filling:

- 2 tablespoons olive oil
- 1 small onion, finely chopped
- 2 garlic cloves, minced
- 1 bell pepper (red or green), finely chopped
- 1/2 cup white wine (optional)
- 1/2 cup heavy cream
- 3 large eggs
- 1 cup milk
- 1 teaspoon dried thyme
- 1 teaspoon dried parsley
- 1/2 teaspoon paprika
- Salt and black pepper to taste
- 1 cup shrimp, peeled and deveined
- 1/2 cup squid rings
- 1/2 cup mussels, cleaned and pre-cooked
- 1/2 cup crab meat (optional)

For Garnish (Optional):

- **Chopped fresh parsley**
- **Lemon wedges**

Instructions:

1. **Prepare the Pastry Crust:**
   - In a large bowl, combine the flour and salt. Cut in the cold butter using a pastry cutter or your fingers until the mixture resembles coarse crumbs.
   - Gradually add the ice water, mixing until the dough just comes together. You may need a little more or less water.

- Form the dough into a disk, wrap it in plastic wrap, and refrigerate for at least 30 minutes.
2. **Preheat the Oven:**
   - Preheat your oven to 375°F (190°C).
3. **Prepare the Filling:**
   - Heat olive oil in a large skillet over medium heat. Add the chopped onion, garlic, and bell pepper, cooking until softened, about 5 minutes.
   - If using white wine, add it to the skillet and cook until it has mostly evaporated.
   - Add the shrimp, squid, mussels, and crab meat (if using). Cook until the seafood is just cooked through. Remove from heat and set aside.
4. **Make the Custard Mixture:**
   - In a large bowl, whisk together the heavy cream, eggs, milk, dried thyme, dried parsley, paprika, salt, and black pepper.
5. **Assemble the Tart:**
   - On a lightly floured surface, roll out the chilled pastry dough to fit a tart pan. Gently press the dough into the pan, trimming any excess.
   - Spread the cooked seafood mixture evenly over the pastry crust.
   - Pour the custard mixture over the seafood, filling the tart almost to the top.
6. **Bake the Tart:**
   - Bake in the preheated oven for 30-40 minutes, or until the filling is set and the top is golden brown.
   - Allow the tart to cool slightly before slicing.
7. **Serve:**
   - Garnish with chopped fresh parsley and lemon wedges if desired. Serve warm or at room temperature.

Tips:

- **Seafood:** You can use any combination of seafood you like, or adjust the quantities based on what's available. Pre-cooked seafood works best for this recipe.
- **Crust:** If you prefer, you can use store-bought pie dough for convenience.
- **Variations:** Feel free to add vegetables like spinach or mushrooms to the filling for extra flavor and texture.

Tarta de Mariscos is a delicious and elegant dish that's sure to impress. Its creamy seafood filling paired with a crisp, buttery crust makes it a perfect choice for a special meal or a festive occasion. Enjoy!

Empanadas de Queso

Ingredients:

For the Dough:

- 2 1/2 cups all-purpose flour
- 1/2 teaspoon salt
- 1/2 cup unsalted butter, cold and cut into small pieces
- 1 large egg
- 1/2 cup cold water (more if needed)
- 1 tablespoon white vinegar (optional, for a flakier dough)

For the Cheese Filling:

- 1 1/2 cups shredded cheese (such as mozzarella, cheddar, or a combination)
- 1/2 cup crumbled feta cheese (optional, for extra flavor)
- 1/4 cup grated Parmesan cheese (optional, for added richness)
- 1 tablespoon chopped fresh parsley or dried oregano (optional)
- Salt and black pepper to taste

For Assembly:

- **1 egg**, beaten (for egg wash)
- **Flour** (for dusting)

Instructions:

1. **Prepare the Dough:**
    - In a large bowl, whisk together the flour and salt.
    - Cut in the cold butter using a pastry cutter or your fingers until the mixture resembles coarse crumbs.
    - In a separate bowl, beat the egg and mix in the cold water and vinegar (if using).
    - Gradually add the wet ingredients to the dry ingredients, mixing until the dough just comes together. You may need to add a bit more water if the dough is too dry.
    - Form the dough into a disk, wrap it in plastic wrap, and refrigerate for at least 30 minutes.
2. **Prepare the Cheese Filling:**
    - In a bowl, combine the shredded cheese, crumbled feta (if using), Parmesan cheese, and chopped parsley or oregano. Season with salt and pepper to taste. Set aside.
3. **Assemble the Empanadas:**

- Preheat your oven to 375°F (190°C) and line a baking sheet with parchment paper.
- On a lightly floured surface, roll out the chilled dough to about 1/8 inch (3 mm) thickness.
- Using a round cutter (about 4-5 inches in diameter), cut out circles of dough.
- Place a tablespoon of the cheese filling in the center of each dough circle.
- Fold the dough over the filling to create a half-moon shape, and press the edges together to seal. You can crimp the edges with a fork or pinch them together for a decorative touch.

4. **Bake the Empanadas:**
   - Place the assembled empanadas on the prepared baking sheet.
   - Brush the tops with the beaten egg for a golden finish.
   - Bake in the preheated oven for 20-25 minutes, or until the empanadas are golden brown and the cheese is melted.

5. **Serve:**
   - Let the empanadas cool slightly before serving. They're delicious warm or at room temperature.

Tips:

- **Cheese Choices:** Feel free to mix and match cheeses according to your preference. Cheese that melts well is ideal.
- **Dough:** If you prefer a shortcut, you can use store-bought empanada dough or pie crust.
- **Frying Option:** For a different texture, you can also fry the empanadas in vegetable oil at 350°F (175°C) until golden and crispy, about 3-4 minutes per side.

Empanadas de Queso are a versatile and crowd-pleasing snack that can be served at parties, gatherings, or as a tasty treat any time. Enjoy making and eating these cheesy delights!

Ceviche Chileno

Ingredients:

- 1 lb (450g) fresh firm white fish (such as hake, sea bass, or tilapia), cut into small cubes
- 1 red onion, thinly sliced
- 1-2 cloves garlic, minced
- 1 cup fresh lemon juice
- 1/2 cup fresh orange juice
- 1-2 tablespoons olive oil
- 1 teaspoon dried oregano
- 1 teaspoon paprika
- 1 teaspoon ground cumin
- Salt and black pepper to taste
- 1 bunch fresh cilantro, chopped
- 1-2 avocados, sliced (for serving)
- 1-2 sweet potatoes, cooked and sliced (for serving)
- Lettuce leaves (for serving, optional)

Instructions:

1. **Prepare the Fish:**
    - Place the fish cubes in a large bowl. Add the minced garlic, dried oregano, paprika, cumin, salt, and black pepper.
    - Pour the fresh lemon and orange juices over the fish. Stir well to ensure the fish is evenly coated.
    - Cover the bowl and refrigerate for at least 1-2 hours. The citrus juices will "cook" the fish, turning it opaque and firm.
2. **Prepare the Vegetables:**
    - Thinly slice the red onion and rinse it under cold water to remove some of its pungency.
    - Add the sliced onion to the fish mixture, stirring to combine.
    - If you like, you can also add some chopped fresh cilantro at this point, or save it for garnish.
3. **Finish the Ceviche:**
    - After the fish has marinated and is fully "cooked" by the citrus, drizzle with olive oil and give it a final stir.
    - Adjust seasoning with more salt, pepper, or additional citrus juice if needed.
4. **Serve:**
    - Serve the ceviche chilled, garnished with additional fresh cilantro if desired.
    - Accompany with sliced avocado, cooked sweet potato slices, and/or lettuce leaves for a traditional presentation.

Tips:

- **Fish Freshness:** Use the freshest fish possible to ensure the best flavor and texture. Sushi-grade fish is ideal.
- **Marinating Time:** The fish needs to marinate long enough to become opaque and firm but avoid over-marinating as it can become too "cooked" and lose its texture.
- **Accompaniments:** Ceviche Chileno is often served with sides like sweet potato and avocado, which balance the tanginess of the dish.

Ceviche Chileno is a light and tangy dish that's perfect for warm weather or as an appetizer. Its combination of fresh fish and citrus flavors makes it a delightful treat that captures the essence of Chilean cuisine. Enjoy!

Tarta de Manzana

Ingredients:

For the Crust:

- 1 1/2 cups all-purpose flour
- 1/2 cup unsalted butter, cold and cut into small pieces
- 1/4 cup granulated sugar
- 1 large egg yolk
- 1-2 tablespoons ice water (more if needed)

For the Filling:

- 4-5 medium apples (such as Granny Smith, Honeycrisp, or a mix), peeled, cored, and thinly sliced
- 1/2 cup granulated sugar
- 1/4 cup brown sugar
- 1 tablespoon all-purpose flour
- 1 teaspoon ground cinnamon
- 1/4 teaspoon ground nutmeg
- 1 tablespoon lemon juice
- 2 tablespoons unsalted butter, cut into small pieces
- 1 egg, beaten (for egg wash)
- Powdered sugar (for dusting, optional)

Instructions:

1. **Prepare the Crust:**
    - In a large bowl, combine the flour and granulated sugar. Cut in the cold butter using a pastry cutter or your fingers until the mixture resembles coarse crumbs.
    - Add the egg yolk and mix until combined. Gradually add the ice water, one tablespoon at a time, until the dough just comes together. You may need more or less water.
    - Form the dough into a disk, wrap it in plastic wrap, and refrigerate for at least 30 minutes.
2. **Prepare the Filling:**
    - In a large bowl, toss the apple slices with granulated sugar, brown sugar, flour, cinnamon, nutmeg, and lemon juice. Set aside.
3. **Assemble the Tart:**
    - Preheat your oven to 375°F (190°C).

- On a lightly floured surface, roll out the chilled dough to fit a tart pan (about 9 inches in diameter). Transfer the dough to the tart pan, pressing it into the bottom and up the sides. Trim any excess dough.
- Arrange the apple slices in the tart shell, overlapping them slightly. Dot the top with small pieces of butter.
- Brush the edges of the crust with the beaten egg to give it a golden finish.

4. **Bake the Tart:**
   - Bake in the preheated oven for 35-45 minutes, or until the apples are tender and the crust is golden brown.
   - If the crust edges start to brown too quickly, cover them with aluminum foil to prevent burning.

5. **Serve:**
   - Allow the tart to cool slightly before serving. Dust with powdered sugar if desired.

Tips:

- **Apple Variety:** Use a mix of apples for a more complex flavor and varied texture. Tart apples like Granny Smith balance the sweetness of the sugar.
- **Crust:** Ensure the butter is very cold to get a flaky texture in the crust.
- **Serving:** Tarta de Manzana is delicious on its own or served with a scoop of vanilla ice cream or a dollop of whipped cream.

Tarta de Manzana is a delightful dessert that brings together the sweetness of apples with the richness of a buttery crust. It's a timeless treat perfect for any occasion. Enjoy!

Pan de Pascua

Ingredients:

For the Cake:

- 2 cups all-purpose flour
- 1 teaspoon baking powder
- 1 teaspoon ground cinnamon
- 1/2 teaspoon ground cloves
- 1/2 teaspoon ground nutmeg
- 1/4 teaspoon salt
- 1 cup unsalted butter, softened
- 1 cup granulated sugar
- 4 large eggs
- 1/2 cup milk
- 1/2 cup orange juice
- 1 cup mixed dried fruits (such as raisins, currants, chopped apricots, and/or dates)
- 1 cup chopped nuts (such as walnuts, almonds, or pecans)
- 1/2 cup candied fruit (such as cherries or citrus peel), chopped
- 1/2 cup dark rum or brandy (optional, for soaking the fruits)
- 1 teaspoon vanilla extract

For the Glaze:

- 1 cup powdered sugar
- 2 tablespoons milk
- 1 tablespoon lemon juice

For Garnish (Optional):

- Candied fruit or marzipan decorations

Instructions:

1. **Prepare the Fruits (Optional):**
   - If using rum or brandy, soak the mixed dried fruits and candied fruit in the alcohol for at least 1 hour or overnight. Drain and set aside.
2. **Prepare the Cake Batter:**
   - Preheat your oven to 350°F (175°C). Grease and flour a 9-inch (23 cm) round cake pan or a loaf pan.
   - In a medium bowl, whisk together the flour, baking powder, cinnamon, cloves, nutmeg, and salt. Set aside.

- In a large bowl, cream the softened butter and granulated sugar until light and fluffy.
- Add the eggs one at a time, beating well after each addition.
- Mix in the vanilla extract.
- Gradually add the flour mixture to the butter mixture, alternating with the milk and orange juice, beginning and ending with the flour mixture. Mix until just combined.
- Fold in the soaked fruits, chopped nuts, and candied fruit.

3. **Bake the Cake:**
   - Pour the batter into the prepared pan and smooth the top with a spatula.
   - Bake in the preheated oven for 50-60 minutes, or until a toothpick inserted into the center comes out clean.
   - Allow the cake to cool in the pan for about 15 minutes, then transfer it to a wire rack to cool completely.

4. **Prepare the Glaze:**
   - In a small bowl, whisk together the powdered sugar, milk, and lemon juice until smooth. Adjust the consistency with more milk or powdered sugar if needed.

5. **Glaze and Garnish the Cake:**
   - Once the cake is completely cooled, drizzle the glaze over the top.
   - Decorate with candied fruit or marzipan decorations if desired.

6. **Serve:**
   - Allow the glaze to set before slicing and serving. Pan de Pascua can be stored in an airtight container at room temperature for up to a week.

Tips:

- **Fruits and Nuts:** Feel free to customize the mix of dried fruits and nuts based on your preference. Toasted nuts can add extra flavor.
- **Alcohol:** The rum or brandy adds depth of flavor but is optional. You can skip it or use orange juice as a substitute for soaking the fruits.
- **Aging:** This cake often tastes even better after a few days, as the flavors meld together.

Pan de Pascua is a festive and flavorful cake that brings together a medley of fruits and spices, making it a perfect treat for the holiday season. Enjoy making and sharing this traditional Chilean Christmas cake!

Torta de Mil Hojas

Ingredients:

For the Pastry:

- 2 1/2 cups all-purpose flour
- 1 cup unsalted butter, cold and cut into small pieces
- 1/2 cup granulated sugar
- 1/2 teaspoon salt
- 1 large egg yolk
- 1/4 cup ice water (more if needed)

For the Filling:

- 1 can (about 14 ounces) dulce de leche (also known as caramel or leche condensada)
- 1 cup heavy cream

For Garnish (Optional):

- **Powdered sugar**
- **Chocolate shavings** or **cocoa powder**

Instructions:

1. **Prepare the Pastry Dough:**
    - In a large bowl, combine the flour, sugar, and salt.
    - Cut in the cold butter using a pastry cutter or your fingers until the mixture resembles coarse crumbs.
    - Add the egg yolk and mix until combined. Gradually add the ice water, one tablespoon at a time, until the dough just comes together. You may need more or less water.
    - Form the dough into a disk, wrap it in plastic wrap, and refrigerate for at least 1 hour.
2. **Roll Out and Bake the Pastry:**
    - Preheat your oven to 375°F (190°C).
    - On a lightly floured surface, roll out the dough into thin sheets, about 1/8 inch (3 mm) thick.
    - Cut the dough into rectangles or circles, depending on your preferred shape for the layers. Transfer them to baking sheets lined with parchment paper.
    - Prick the dough with a fork to prevent puffing.
    - Bake in the preheated oven for 10-12 minutes, or until the pastry is golden and crisp.

- Allow the baked pastry layers to cool completely on a wire rack.
3. **Prepare the Filling:**
   - Whip the heavy cream until soft peaks form.
   - Fold the whipped cream into the dulce de leche until well combined.
4. **Assemble the Cake:**
   - Spread a thin layer of the dulce de leche filling onto one pastry layer.
   - Place another pastry layer on top and repeat the process, building up the layers.
   - Finish with a final layer of pastry on top.
   - Optionally, you can spread a thin layer of filling on the top and sides of the cake, smoothing it out.
5. **Garnish:**
   - Dust the top of the cake with powdered sugar or cocoa powder.
   - Add chocolate shavings or other decorations if desired.
6. **Serve:**
   - Chill the assembled cake in the refrigerator for at least 1 hour to let the flavors meld and the filling set.
   - Slice and serve chilled.

Tips:

- **Chilling the Dough:** Keeping the dough cold helps maintain its flakiness.
- **Layering:** Ensure that each layer is even and crisp for the best texture. If the pastry layers are uneven, the cake might be harder to assemble.
- **Filling Variations:** You can experiment with different fillings, such as pastry cream or fruit preserves, if you prefer a variation on the classic dulce de leche.

Torta de Mil Hojas is a show-stopping dessert with its rich, caramel filling and crisp pastry layers. It's perfect for special occasions and will impress anyone who loves a sweet, decadent treat. Enjoy!

Lomo a lo Pobre

Ingredients:

For the Steak:

- 4 beef sirloin steaks (about 6-8 oz each)
- 2 tablespoons vegetable oil or olive oil
- Salt and black pepper, to taste
- 2 cloves garlic, minced (optional)
- 1 tablespoon fresh rosemary or thyme (optional)

For the Fries:

- 4 large potatoes, peeled and cut into fries
- Vegetable oil, for frying
- Salt, to taste

For the Toppings:

- 4 large eggs
- 1 large onion, thinly sliced
- 2 tablespoons vegetable oil (for frying onions)
- 1 tablespoon chopped fresh parsley (for garnish, optional)

For Serving (Optional):

- Avocado slices
- Tomato salad or lettuce

Instructions:

1. **Prepare the Fries:**
    - Peel and cut the potatoes into thin strips for fries.
    - Rinse the potato strips in cold water to remove excess starch, then pat them dry with paper towels.
    - Heat vegetable oil in a deep fryer or large heavy-bottomed pot to 350°F (175°C).
    - Fry the potato strips in batches until they are golden brown and crispy, about 3-5 minutes per batch.
    - Remove the fries with a slotted spoon and drain on paper towels. Season with salt immediately.
2. **Cook the Steak:**
    - Season the beef steaks with salt, black pepper, and minced garlic if using.
    - Heat vegetable oil in a large skillet over medium-high heat.

- Cook the steaks to your desired level of doneness, about 4-5 minutes per side for medium-rare, depending on thickness.
- Optionally, add fresh rosemary or thyme to the skillet while cooking for added flavor.
- Remove the steaks from the skillet and let them rest for a few minutes.
3. **Prepare the Onions:**
   - In the same skillet, add a bit more oil if needed and sauté the sliced onions over medium heat until they are caramelized and golden brown, about 10 minutes. Set aside.
4. **Fry the Eggs:**
   - In a separate non-stick skillet, heat a little oil over medium heat.
   - Fry the eggs sunny-side up or to your desired doneness.
5. **Assemble the Dish:**
   - On each plate, arrange a portion of fries.
   - Place a cooked steak on top of the fries.
   - Top the steak with caramelized onions.
   - Place a fried egg on top of the steak and onions.
   - Garnish with chopped parsley if desired.
6. **Serve:**
   - Serve **Lomo a lo Pobre** immediately while everything is warm.
   - Optionally, you can also serve it with slices of avocado and a side salad for added freshness.

Tips:

- **Steak:** Adjust the cooking time based on your preferred steak doneness. Use a meat thermometer if needed.
- **Fries:** For extra crispy fries, double-fry them—first at a lower temperature, then at a higher temperature.
- **Eggs:** Sunny-side up eggs are traditional, but you can cook them to your liking.

Lomo a lo Pobre is a robust, comforting dish that combines a juicy steak with crispy fries and a flavorful egg topping. It's a great choice for a hearty meal that captures the essence of Chilean comfort food. Enjoy!

Arroz con Pollo

Ingredients:

- 1 whole chicken, cut into pieces (or 4-6 bone-in, skinless chicken thighs and/or drumsticks)
- 2 tablespoons vegetable oil or olive oil
- 1 medium onion, finely chopped
- 1 red bell pepper, diced
- 2 garlic cloves, minced
- 1 cup frozen peas
- 1 cup carrots, diced (or 1 cup frozen carrots)
- 2 cups long-grain rice (like Basmati or Jasmine)
- 1/4 cup tomato paste or 1 cup diced tomatoes
- 2 1/2 cups chicken broth (or water)
- 1/2 cup white wine (optional)
- 1 teaspoon ground cumin
- 1 teaspoon paprika
- 1/2 teaspoon turmeric (for color)
- 1 bay leaf
- Salt and black pepper, to taste
- 1/4 cup chopped fresh cilantro (for garnish)
- 1 lemon or lime, cut into wedges (for serving)

Instructions:

1. **Prepare the Chicken:**
    - Season the chicken pieces with salt and black pepper.
    - Heat the oil in a large, deep skillet or Dutch oven over medium-high heat.
    - Brown the chicken pieces on all sides until golden, about 5-7 minutes per side. Remove the chicken and set aside.
2. **Cook the Vegetables:**
    - In the same skillet, add the chopped onion and red bell pepper. Sauté until softened, about 5 minutes.
    - Add the minced garlic and cook for another minute.
3. **Prepare the Rice Mixture:**
    - Stir in the tomato paste (or diced tomatoes) and cook for 2-3 minutes to combine flavors.
    - Add the rice and stir to coat with the tomato mixture.
    - Pour in the chicken broth and white wine (if using). Stir in the cumin, paprika, turmeric, and bay leaf.
4. **Combine and Cook:**

- Return the browned chicken pieces to the skillet, placing them on top of the rice mixture.
- Bring the mixture to a boil, then reduce the heat to low.
- Cover the skillet with a lid and simmer for 20-25 minutes, or until the rice is cooked and the chicken is tender.
- About 10 minutes before the cooking time is up, add the frozen peas and carrots, stirring gently to combine.

5. **Finish and Serve:**
   - Once the rice and chicken are cooked, remove from heat and let the dish sit, covered, for 5 minutes.
   - Discard the bay leaf and adjust seasoning with more salt and pepper if needed.
   - Garnish with chopped fresh cilantro.
   - Serve with lemon or lime wedges for added flavor.

Tips:

- **Chicken:** Bone-in, skinless chicken thighs or drumsticks work well because they stay moist during cooking. You can also use boneless chicken pieces, but they may cook faster.
- **Rice:** Make sure not to stir the rice too much once it's added, as this can make it sticky.
- **Vegetables:** Feel free to customize the vegetables based on what you have on hand or your preferences.
- **Flavor:** For additional flavor, you can add a pinch of saffron or a splash of hot sauce.

Arroz con Pollo is a comforting and flavorful dish that's perfect for family gatherings and weeknight dinners. Its combination of tender chicken, savory rice, and vegetables makes it a complete and satisfying meal. Enjoy!

Zapallo Italiano Relleno

Ingredients:

- 4 medium-sized zucchini or Italian squash
- 1 tablespoon olive oil
- 1 onion, finely chopped
- 2 garlic cloves, minced
- 1 bell pepper, finely chopped (any color)
- 1 cup ground beef or ground turkey (can substitute with vegetarian ground meat)
- 1 cup cooked rice (optional, for added texture)
- 1 cup grated cheese (such as mozzarella, cheddar, or a blend)
- 1/2 cup tomato sauce or diced tomatoes
- 1 teaspoon dried oregano
- 1/2 teaspoon ground cumin
- 1/2 teaspoon paprika
- Salt and black pepper, to taste
- Fresh parsley or basil (for garnish, optional)

Instructions:

1. **Prepare the Zucchini:**
    - Preheat your oven to 375°F (190°C).
    - Cut the ends off the zucchini and slice them in half lengthwise.
    - Using a spoon or melon baller, scoop out the seeds and some of the flesh to create boats. Set aside the scooped flesh.
2. **Prepare the Filling:**
    - Heat olive oil in a large skillet over medium heat.
    - Add the chopped onion and bell pepper and sauté until softened, about 5 minutes.
    - Add the minced garlic and cook for another minute.
    - Stir in the ground beef (or turkey) and cook until browned and fully cooked. Break up any large chunks with a spoon.
    - Add the reserved zucchini flesh to the skillet and cook until it is tender.
    - Mix in the tomato sauce (or diced tomatoes), cooked rice (if using), oregano, cumin, paprika, salt, and black pepper. Stir well and cook for a few more minutes until everything is well combined and heated through.
3. **Stuff the Zucchini:**
    - Place the hollowed-out zucchini halves in a baking dish.
    - Spoon the filling mixture into each zucchini boat, packing it in well.
    - Sprinkle the grated cheese evenly over the top of each stuffed zucchini.
4. **Bake:**

- Cover the baking dish with aluminum foil and bake in the preheated oven for 20 minutes.
- Remove the foil and bake for an additional 10-15 minutes, or until the zucchini is tender and the cheese is melted and bubbly.

5. **Garnish and Serve:**
   - Garnish with chopped fresh parsley or basil if desired.
   - Serve hot, either as a main dish or a side dish.

Tips:

- **Zucchini Size:** Choose medium-sized zucchinis that are firm and not overly large, as they will hold their shape better and cook more evenly.
- **Filling Variations:** Feel free to customize the filling with additional vegetables like mushrooms, spinach, or corn, or add spices to taste.
- **Cheese:** Use your favorite cheese or a blend for a richer flavor.

Zapallo Italiano Relleno is a versatile and satisfying dish that's perfect for family dinners or entertaining. The combination of tender zucchini and flavorful filling makes it a delicious and nutritious option. Enjoy!

Ensalada de Palta

Ingredients:

- 3 ripe avocados
- 1 small red onion, finely chopped
- 1-2 medium tomatoes, diced
- 1 small cucumber, peeled and diced (optional)
- 1/4 cup fresh cilantro, chopped (optional)
- 1-2 tablespoons fresh lime juice or lemon juice
- 2 tablespoons olive oil
- Salt and black pepper, to taste

Instructions:

1. **Prepare the Avocados:**
   - Cut the avocados in half and remove the pit.
   - Scoop the flesh out of the skins with a spoon and cut it into bite-sized cubes.
2. **Prepare the Vegetables:**
   - In a large bowl, combine the chopped red onion, diced tomatoes, and cucumber (if using).
   - Gently fold in the avocado cubes.
3. **Dress the Salad:**
   - Drizzle the olive oil and fresh lime (or lemon) juice over the salad.
   - Season with salt and black pepper to taste.
   - Add chopped cilantro if using, and toss gently to combine.
4. **Serve:**
   - Serve the salad immediately for the freshest taste. If you need to prepare it in advance, be sure to add the avocado just before serving to prevent it from browning.

Tips:

- **Avocado Ripeness:** Make sure your avocados are ripe but still firm to the touch to prevent them from becoming mushy.
- **Variations:** You can customize this salad by adding ingredients like sliced radishes, crumbled feta cheese, or a sprinkle of chili flakes for extra flavor.
- **Freshness:** Avocado can brown quickly, so try to serve the salad soon after preparing it. If you need to store it, place plastic wrap directly on the surface of the salad to minimize oxidation.

Ensalada de Palta is a versatile and delicious salad that showcases the creamy richness of avocados. It pairs wonderfully with a variety of main dishes and is perfect for warm weather or as a fresh, light side at any meal. Enjoy!

Puchero

Ingredients:

For the Stew:

- **2 lbs (900g) beef shank** or **beef chuck**, cut into chunks
- **1/2 lb (225g) pork ribs** or **pork shoulder**, cut into chunks (optional)
- **1 onion**, peeled and halved
- **2 cloves garlic**, peeled
- **2 bay leaves**
- **1 teaspoon dried oregano**
- **1 teaspoon paprika**
- **Salt and black pepper**, to taste
- **1-2 medium carrots**, peeled and cut into large chunks
- **1-2 potatoes**, peeled and cut into large chunks
- **1 cup dried chickpeas** (soaked overnight) or **1 can chickpeas**, drained and rinsed
- **1-2 cups cabbage**, cut into wedges
- **1-2 corn cobs**, cut into chunks (optional)

For Garnish (Optional):

- **Chimichurri sauce** or **salsa** for serving

Instructions:

1. **Prepare the Meat:**
   - In a large pot or Dutch oven, add the beef shank and pork ribs (if using). Cover with water and bring to a boil.
   - Once boiling, reduce the heat to a simmer and skim off any foam that rises to the surface.
   - Add the onion, garlic, bay leaves, oregano, paprika, salt, and black pepper.
   - Cover and simmer for about 1-1.5 hours, or until the meat is tender.
2. **Add the Vegetables:**
   - Add the carrots, potatoes, and soaked chickpeas (or canned chickpeas) to the pot. Stir well.
   - Continue to simmer for another 30-40 minutes, or until the vegetables are tender.
3. **Add the Cabbage and Corn:**
   - Add the cabbage and corn chunks (if using) to the pot. Stir gently.
   - Simmer for an additional 15-20 minutes, or until the cabbage and corn are cooked.
4. **Adjust Seasoning:**
   - Taste the broth and adjust seasoning with more salt and pepper if needed.

5. **Serve:**
    - Remove the meat and vegetables from the pot and place them on a serving platter.
    - Serve the stew with a side of chimichurri sauce or salsa if desired.

Tips:

- **Meat:** You can use a combination of beef and pork, or just one type of meat. The key is to use cuts that will become tender after long, slow cooking.
- **Chickpeas:** If using dried chickpeas, make sure to soak them overnight and cook them with the stew. Canned chickpeas can be added later in the cooking process.
- **Vegetables:** Feel free to add other vegetables like turnips or parsnips according to your preference.

Puchero is a versatile and satisfying stew that showcases the rich flavors of slowly cooked meat and vegetables. It's a great way to bring comfort and warmth to any meal, especially on a chilly day. Enjoy!

Sopaipillas Pasadas

Ingredients:

For the Sopaipillas:

- 2 cups all-purpose flour
- 1/2 teaspoon baking powder
- 1/2 teaspoon salt
- 1/2 teaspoon ground cinnamon (optional)
- 1/2 cup unsalted butter, cold and cut into small pieces
- 1/2 cup pumpkin puree (can use butternut squash as a substitute)
- 1/4 cup cold water (more if needed)
- Vegetable oil, for frying

For the Syrup:

- 1 cup raw sugar or brown sugar
- 1 cup water
- 1 cinnamon stick
- 1-2 cloves
- 1 tablespoon lemon juice (optional, for a slight tang)
- 1 tablespoon cornstarch (optional, for thickening)

Instructions:

1. **Prepare the Dough:**
    - In a large bowl, combine the flour, baking powder, salt, and ground cinnamon if using.
    - Cut in the cold butter with a pastry cutter or your fingers until the mixture resembles coarse crumbs.
    - Add the pumpkin puree and mix until combined.
    - Gradually add cold water, a tablespoon at a time, until the dough comes together. The dough should be soft but not sticky. If necessary, add a bit more flour if the dough is too sticky.
2. **Roll and Cut:**
    - On a lightly floured surface, roll out the dough to about 1/4-inch thickness.
    - Cut the dough into 2-inch squares or rounds, using a knife or cookie cutter.
3. **Fry the Sopaipillas:**
    - Heat vegetable oil in a deep skillet or pot to 350°F (175°C).
    - Fry the sopaipillas in batches, being careful not to overcrowd the pan. Fry them until golden brown and puffed up, about 2-3 minutes per side.

- Use a slotted spoon to transfer the fried sopaipillas to a plate lined with paper towels to drain excess oil.
4. **Prepare the Syrup:**
    - In a saucepan, combine the sugar, water, cinnamon stick, cloves, and lemon juice (if using).
    - Bring to a boil, stirring occasionally until the sugar is dissolved.
    - Reduce the heat and let it simmer for about 10 minutes. If you prefer a thicker syrup, dissolve cornstarch in a little cold water and add it to the syrup, cooking until thickened.
5. **Coat the Sopaipillas:**
    - While still warm, dip each sopaipilla into the syrup, making sure to coat both sides. Allow any excess syrup to drip off before serving.
6. **Serve:**
    - Serve the sopaipillas warm or at room temperature. They're often enjoyed with a cup of tea or coffee.

Tips:

- **Pumpkin Puree:** You can make your own pumpkin puree by roasting and blending pumpkin or butternut squash, or use canned pumpkin puree.
- **Syrup Consistency:** Adjust the thickness of the syrup according to your preference. For a thicker syrup, let it simmer longer or use cornstarch.
- **Storage:** Sopaipillas Pasadas are best enjoyed fresh, but you can store them in an airtight container for a day or two. Reheat them slightly before serving if needed.

Sopaipillas Pasadas are a delightful and comforting treat with their sweet, syrupy coating and soft, airy interior. They make a wonderful dessert for gatherings or a special treat for yourself. Enjoy!

Relleno de Pavo

Ingredients:

For the Turkey:

- 1 whole turkey (12-14 lbs), thawed if frozen
- Salt and black pepper, to taste
- 2 tablespoons olive oil or butter, melted

For the Stuffing:

- 1 loaf of day-old bread, cut into cubes (about 6-8 cups)
- 1 large onion, finely chopped
- 2 celery stalks, finely chopped
- 2 cloves garlic, minced
- 1 cup chicken or turkey broth (more if needed)
- 1/2 cup dried cranberries or raisins (optional)
- 1/2 cup chopped nuts (such as walnuts or pecans, optional)
- 2 tablespoons fresh sage, chopped (or 1 tablespoon dried sage)
- 1 tablespoon fresh thyme, chopped (or 1 teaspoon dried thyme)
- 1 tablespoon fresh rosemary, chopped (or 1 teaspoon dried rosemary)
- 1 teaspoon ground cinnamon (optional)
- 1/2 teaspoon ground nutmeg (optional)
- 2 tablespoons butter
- Salt and black pepper, to taste

Instructions:

1. **Prepare the Stuffing:**
    - In a large skillet, melt the butter over medium heat.
    - Add the chopped onion, celery, and garlic. Sauté until the vegetables are softened, about 5-7 minutes.
    - In a large bowl, combine the bread cubes, sautéed vegetables, dried cranberries (if using), nuts (if using), and chopped herbs.
    - Pour in the chicken or turkey broth, a little at a time, until the bread is moist but not soggy. Mix gently to combine.
    - Season with salt, black pepper, cinnamon, and nutmeg, if using. Adjust seasoning to taste.
2. **Prepare the Turkey:**
    - Preheat your oven to 325°F (165°C).
    - Remove the giblets and neck from the turkey cavity and pat the turkey dry with paper towels.

- Season the turkey inside and out with salt and black pepper.
- Stuff the turkey cavity with the prepared stuffing, packing it in lightly. If there is leftover stuffing, you can place it in a baking dish and bake it alongside the turkey.

3. **Roast the Turkey:**
   - Place the stuffed turkey on a rack in a roasting pan.
   - Brush the turkey with melted olive oil or butter.
   - Cover the turkey loosely with aluminum foil to prevent excessive browning.
   - Roast the turkey in the preheated oven. The general rule is about 15 minutes per pound. For a 12-14 lb turkey, this will be approximately 3 to 4 hours.
   - Remove the foil during the last 30-45 minutes of cooking to allow the skin to brown and become crispy.
   - The turkey is done when the internal temperature reaches 165°F (74°C) in the thickest part of the thigh and the stuffing reaches 165°F (74°C) as well.

4. **Rest and Serve:**
   - Once the turkey is cooked, remove it from the oven and let it rest for 20-30 minutes before carving. This helps the juices redistribute throughout the meat.
   - If you have extra stuffing in a separate dish, bake it at 325°F (165°C) for about 30 minutes, or until heated through.

5. **Carve and Enjoy:**
   - Carve the turkey and serve with the stuffing and your favorite sides.

Tips:

- **Stuffing:** Avoid overstuffing the turkey to ensure even cooking. If necessary, cook any extra stuffing in a separate dish.
- **Basting:** Baste the turkey occasionally with its own juices or additional melted butter to keep it moist.
- **Resting Time:** Letting the turkey rest before carving allows the meat to retain its juices, making it more flavorful and tender.

Relleno de Pavo is a classic and festive dish that's perfect for celebrations and special occasions. The savory stuffing and perfectly roasted turkey create a delicious and memorable meal. Enjoy your holiday feast!

Calzones Rotos

Ingredients:

- 2 1/2 cups all-purpose flour
- 1/2 cup granulated sugar
- 1/2 teaspoon baking powder
- 1/4 teaspoon salt
- 1/2 cup unsalted butter, cold and cut into small pieces
- 2 large eggs
- 1 tablespoon brandy or rum (optional, for added flavor)
- Vegetable oil, for frying
- Powdered sugar, for dusting

Instructions:

1. **Prepare the Dough:**
    - In a large bowl, whisk together the flour, granulated sugar, baking powder, and salt.
    - Cut in the cold butter using a pastry cutter or your fingers until the mixture resembles coarse crumbs.
    - In a separate bowl, beat the eggs and mix in the brandy or rum if using.
    - Pour the egg mixture into the flour mixture and stir until a dough forms. You may need to add a little more flour if the dough is too sticky.
    - Turn the dough onto a lightly floured surface and knead briefly until smooth. Wrap it in plastic wrap and refrigerate for at least 30 minutes.
2. **Roll and Cut:**
    - On a lightly floured surface, roll out the dough to about 1/8-inch thickness.
    - Cut the dough into rectangles or squares, about 3-4 inches in size. You can also make traditional diamond shapes by cutting the rectangles diagonally.
3. **Fry the Calzones:**
    - Heat vegetable oil in a deep skillet or pot to 350°F (175°C).
    - Fry the dough pieces in batches, being careful not to overcrowd the pan. Cook until they are golden brown and crispy, about 1-2 minutes per side.
    - Use a slotted spoon to transfer the fried calzones to a plate lined with paper towels to drain excess oil.
4. **Dust and Serve:**
    - Once the calzones are cool enough to handle, dust them generously with powdered sugar.
    - Serve at room temperature. They are best enjoyed fresh but can be stored in an airtight container for a few days.

Tips:

- **Rolling the Dough:** Keep the dough well-floured while rolling out to prevent sticking.
- **Frying:** Maintain the oil temperature to ensure even cooking. If the oil is too hot, the calzones may burn; if too cool, they may become greasy.
- **Flavor Variations:** You can add a bit of cinnamon to the dough or incorporate lemon or orange zest for extra flavor.

Calzones Rotos are a wonderful treat with their crispy texture and sweet powdered sugar coating. They bring a touch of Chilean tradition to your table and are perfect for sharing with family and friends. Enjoy!

Leche Asada

Ingredients:

- 1 can (14 oz) sweetened condensed milk
- 1 can (12 oz) evaporated milk
- 4 large eggs
- 1 cup whole milk
- 1 cup granulated sugar
- 1 teaspoon vanilla extract
- 1/4 teaspoon ground cinnamon (optional)

Instructions:

1. **Prepare the Caramel:**
   - In a medium saucepan over medium heat, cook the granulated sugar until it melts and turns a deep amber color. This should take about 5-7 minutes. Stir occasionally to ensure even melting, but avoid stirring too much once it starts to caramelize.
   - Once the sugar is fully melted and golden brown, pour it into a baking dish (approximately 9x13 inches or similar) and swirl to coat the bottom evenly. Set aside to cool and harden.
2. **Prepare the Custard Mixture:**
   - In a large bowl, whisk together the sweetened condensed milk, evaporated milk, whole milk, eggs, vanilla extract, and ground cinnamon (if using).
   - Ensure the mixture is well combined and smooth.
3. **Bake the Dessert:**
   - Preheat your oven to 350°F (175°C).
   - Pour the custard mixture over the caramelized sugar in the baking dish.
   - Place the baking dish in a larger roasting pan. Fill the roasting pan with hot water until it comes halfway up the sides of the baking dish. This water bath helps cook the custard evenly and prevents it from cracking.
4. **Bake:**
   - Bake in the preheated oven for about 50-60 minutes, or until the custard is set. You can check for doneness by inserting a knife or toothpick into the center; it should come out clean or with just a few moist crumbs.
   - The top should be slightly browned and the custard should be firm but still a bit jiggly in the center.
5. **Cool and Serve:**
   - Remove the baking dish from the water bath and let it cool to room temperature.
   - Once cooled, refrigerate the Leche Asada for at least 4 hours or overnight to allow it to fully set and develop its flavors.

- To serve, run a knife around the edges of the custard to loosen it, then invert onto a serving platter. The caramel should now be on top, creating a glossy, sweet layer.

Tips:

- **Caramel:** Be cautious when melting the sugar as it can quickly go from caramelized to burnt. Once the sugar starts to melt, watch it closely and stir gently if needed.
- **Water Bath:** Using a water bath is crucial for even cooking. Make sure the water doesn't get into the custard mixture.
- **Serving:** Leche Asada can be served chilled or at room temperature, depending on your preference.

Leche Asada is a simple yet elegant dessert that offers a lovely balance of creamy custard and rich caramel. It's a great way to end a meal with a touch of Chilean tradition. Enjoy!

Mote con Huesillos

Ingredients:

For the Huesillos:

- 1 cup dried peaches (huesillos)
- 1/2 cup sugar (adjust to taste)
- 1 cinnamon stick
- 2-3 whole cloves
- 1-2 cups water (or enough to cover the peaches)

For the Mote:

- 1 cup dried wheat kernels (mote)
- 1/2 teaspoon salt
- 4 cups water

For the Drink:

- 4 cups water (for the final drink mixture)
- 1/2 cup sugar (or to taste)
- Juice of 1 lemon (or lime, optional)
- Ice cubes (optional, for serving)

Instructions:

1. **Prepare the Huesillos:**
    - In a medium pot, combine the dried peaches, sugar, cinnamon stick, cloves, and enough water to cover the peaches.
    - Bring to a boil, then reduce heat and simmer for about 30-40 minutes, or until the peaches are tender and the syrup has thickened slightly.
    - Remove from heat and let it cool. Once cooled, discard the cinnamon stick and cloves.
2. **Prepare the Mote:**
    - Rinse the dried wheat kernels under cold water.
    - In a large pot, combine the wheat, salt, and 4 cups of water.
    - Bring to a boil, then reduce heat and simmer for about 1-1.5 hours, or until the wheat is tender. You may need to add more water during cooking to keep the wheat covered.
    - Once cooked, drain the wheat and let it cool.
3. **Combine and Chill:**

        - In a large pitcher, mix the cooked wheat (mote) with the cooled peach syrup and peaches.
        - Add 4 cups of water and stir well. Adjust sweetness with additional sugar if needed.
        - Add lemon or lime juice to taste, if desired.
        - Chill the mixture in the refrigerator for at least 2 hours, or until well chilled.
4. **Serve:**
        - Serve the Mote con Huesillos over ice if you prefer it extra cold.
        - Pour into glasses with some of the peach slices and cooked wheat included in each serving.

Tips:

- **Adjust Sweetness:** The sweetness of the drink can be adjusted to your taste by adding more or less sugar.
- **Consistency:** If the syrup becomes too thick after chilling, you can add a little more water to achieve your desired consistency.
- **Variations:** Some recipes include additional spices like star anise or a splash of white wine for added complexity.

Mote con Huesillos is not only a refreshing and unique drink but also a cultural staple in Chile. It's a great way to enjoy a combination of fruit and grain in a deliciously sweet and cooling form. Enjoy this delightful treat during warm weather or any time you crave something different!

Pionono

Ingredients:

For the Sponge Cake:

- 4 large eggs
- 1 cup granulated sugar
- 1 teaspoon vanilla extract
- 1 cup all-purpose flour
- 1 teaspoon baking powder
- 1/4 teaspoon salt

For the Filling (Dulce de Leche):

- **1 can (14 oz) dulce de leche** (or homemade caramel sauce)
- **1/2 cup heavy cream** (optional, for a lighter filling)

For the Frosting (Optional):

- **1 cup heavy cream**
- **2 tablespoons powdered sugar**
- **1 teaspoon vanilla extract**

Instructions:

1. **Prepare the Sponge Cake:**
    - Preheat your oven to 375°F (190°C). Line a 15x10-inch jelly roll pan with parchment paper, and lightly grease the parchment paper.
    - In a large bowl, beat the eggs and granulated sugar together with an electric mixer on high speed until thick and pale, about 5 minutes. Add the vanilla extract and mix well.
    - In a separate bowl, sift together the flour, baking powder, and salt. Gently fold the dry ingredients into the egg mixture, being careful not to deflate the batter.
    - Pour the batter into the prepared pan and spread it evenly. Bake in the preheated oven for 10-12 minutes, or until the cake is lightly golden and springs back when touched.
    - While the cake is baking, prepare a clean kitchen towel and sprinkle it with powdered sugar.
    - Once baked, immediately turn the cake out onto the prepared towel. Carefully peel off the parchment paper. Starting from one end, roll the cake up with the towel while it's still warm, and let it cool completely in this rolled position.
2. **Prepare the Filling:**

- If using dulce de leche straight from the can, you can use it as is or lighten it by mixing it with heavy cream until it reaches a spreadable consistency.
- If you want to use a different filling, you can substitute with whipped cream, fruit preserves, or chocolate ganache.

3. **Assemble the Pionono:**
    - Once the cake is completely cool, unroll it gently and spread the filling evenly over the surface.
    - Re-roll the cake carefully without the towel, creating a tight roll. Place the seam side down on a serving platter.
4. **Prepare the Frosting (Optional):**
    - In a chilled bowl, beat the heavy cream with an electric mixer until it starts to thicken. Add the powdered sugar and vanilla extract, and continue to beat until soft peaks form.
    - Spread or pipe the whipped cream over the top of the rolled cake.
5. **Serve:**
    - Slice the Pionono into pieces and serve. It can be garnished with fresh fruit, chocolate shavings, or a dusting of powdered sugar if desired.

Tips:

- **Cake Roll:** Be gentle when rolling the cake to avoid cracks. It's helpful to use a thin, flexible spatula to spread the filling.
- **Chilling:** If using a lighter filling or frosting, chill the Pionono for about 30 minutes before serving to help it set.
- **Variations:** Experiment with different fillings and frostings to suit your taste. You can also add a layer of fruit preserves or chocolate ganache under the filling for extra flavor.

Pionono is a versatile and delicious dessert that's sure to impress. Whether you stick with the classic dulce de leche filling or get creative with different flavors, it's a treat that's perfect for any occasion. Enjoy!

Salmón a la Parrilla

Ingredients:

- 4 salmon fillets (about 6 oz each), skin-on
- 2 tablespoons olive oil
- 1 lemon, cut into wedges
- 2 cloves garlic, minced
- 1 tablespoon fresh dill or parsley, chopped (or 1 teaspoon dried dill)
- Salt and black pepper, to taste
- 1 teaspoon paprika (optional, for extra flavor)
- 1 teaspoon lemon zest (optional, for added brightness)

Instructions:

1. **Prepare the Salmon:**
   - Pat the salmon fillets dry with paper towels. This helps to achieve a crispy skin.
   - Brush both sides of the salmon with olive oil. Season the fillets generously with salt and black pepper. If using, sprinkle paprika and lemon zest over the fillets.
   - Rub the minced garlic and chopped fresh dill or parsley onto the fillets for additional flavor.
2. **Preheat the Grill:**
   - Preheat your grill to medium-high heat (about 400°F or 200°C). Make sure the grates are clean and lightly oiled to prevent sticking.
3. **Grill the Salmon:**
   - Place the salmon fillets on the grill, skin side down. Close the lid and grill for about 4-6 minutes per side, depending on the thickness of the fillets.
     - For fillets that are 1-inch thick, grill for about 4-6 minutes on each side.
     - For fillets that are thicker or thinner, adjust the cooking time accordingly.
   - Avoid moving the fillets too much to ensure the skin becomes crispy. Use a fish spatula to carefully flip the fillets.
4. **Check for Doneness:**
   - The salmon is done when it easily flakes with a fork and reaches an internal temperature of 145°F (63°C). The flesh should be opaque and moist.
5. **Serve:**
   - Remove the salmon from the grill and let it rest for a few minutes.
   - Serve with lemon wedges on the side for squeezing over the top. This adds a fresh, tangy flavor to the grilled salmon.

Tips:

- **Grilling Skin-On:** Keeping the skin on helps protect the delicate flesh and adds flavor. It also helps keep the fillets together during grilling.
- **Marinating:** If you prefer, you can marinate the salmon in a mixture of olive oil, lemon juice, garlic, and herbs for about 30 minutes before grilling for extra flavor.
- **Avoid Overcooking:** Salmon cooks quickly, so keep an eye on it to avoid overcooking. It's better to slightly undercook the fish, as it will continue to cook slightly from residual heat after being removed from the grill.

Salmón a la Parrilla is a straightforward and elegant dish that's perfect for a summer barbecue or a healthy weeknight dinner. The smoky char from the grill complements the rich, buttery flavor of the salmon beautifully. Enjoy your meal!

Ensalada de Porotos

Ingredients:

- 2 cups cooked beans (such as black beans, kidney beans, or pinto beans; if using canned, drain and rinse them)
- 1 cup cherry tomatoes, halved
- 1/2 red onion, finely chopped
- 1 cucumber, diced
- 1/2 cup bell pepper, diced (red, yellow, or green)
- 1/4 cup fresh parsley or cilantro, chopped
- 1 avocado, diced (optional)
- 1/4 cup olives, sliced (optional)

For the Dressing:

- 1/4 cup olive oil
- 2 tablespoons red wine vinegar or lemon juice
- 1 clove garlic, minced
- 1 teaspoon Dijon mustard (optional)
- 1/2 teaspoon ground cumin (optional)
- Salt and black pepper, to taste

Instructions:

1. **Prepare the Ingredients:**
    - If using dried beans, soak and cook them according to package instructions. If using canned beans, drain and rinse them under cold water.
    - Prepare the vegetables by chopping and dicing them as needed.
2. **Mix the Salad:**
    - In a large bowl, combine the cooked beans, cherry tomatoes, red onion, cucumber, bell pepper, and fresh parsley or cilantro.
    - Gently fold in the avocado and olives if using.
3. **Prepare the Dressing:**
    - In a small bowl or jar, whisk together the olive oil, red wine vinegar (or lemon juice), minced garlic, Dijon mustard (if using), and ground cumin (if using). Season with salt and black pepper to taste.
4. **Combine and Serve:**
    - Pour the dressing over the bean mixture and toss gently to coat all the ingredients evenly.
    - Taste and adjust seasoning if needed. Let the salad sit for at least 15-30 minutes before serving to allow the flavors to meld.
5. **Serve:**

- Serve the salad chilled or at room temperature. It's a great accompaniment to grilled meats, or it can be enjoyed on its own as a light meal.

Tips:

- **Bean Variety:** You can use a single type of bean or a mix of different beans. Canned beans are convenient and work well, but dried beans offer a richer flavor and texture.
- **Additional Ingredients:** Feel free to add other ingredients like corn, radishes, or shredded cheese to customize the salad to your taste.
- **Make Ahead:** This salad keeps well in the refrigerator for a couple of days, making it an excellent option for meal prep.

Ensalada de Porotos is a refreshing and filling dish that brings together a variety of textures and flavors. It's perfect for a summer picnic, a potluck, or as a healthy addition to any meal. Enjoy!

Tarta de Dulce de Leche

Ingredients:

For the Tart Shell:

- 1 1/2 cups all-purpose flour
- 1/2 cup powdered sugar
- 1/2 cup unsalted butter, cold and cut into small pieces
- 1 large egg yolk
- 1-2 tablespoons cold water

For the Dulce de Leche Filling:

- 1 can (14 oz) dulce de leche (store-bought or homemade)
- 1 cup heavy cream
- 1 teaspoon vanilla extract

For Garnish (Optional):

- Whipped cream
- Shaved chocolate or cocoa powder
- Fresh fruit (such as strawberries or raspberries)

Instructions:

1. **Prepare the Tart Shell:**
   - In a food processor, combine the flour and powdered sugar. Add the cold butter and pulse until the mixture resembles coarse crumbs.
   - Add the egg yolk and pulse to combine. If the dough seems too dry, add cold water, one tablespoon at a time, until the dough comes together.
   - Turn the dough out onto a lightly floured surface and knead it gently to bring it together. Flatten it into a disc, wrap it in plastic wrap, and refrigerate for at least 30 minutes.
2. **Preheat the Oven:**
   - Preheat your oven to 375°F (190°C).
3. **Roll and Bake the Tart Shell:**
   - On a lightly floured surface, roll out the chilled dough to about 1/8-inch thickness. Carefully transfer the dough to a tart pan (about 9 inches in diameter) with a removable bottom, pressing it into the edges.
   - Trim any excess dough and prick the bottom of the tart shell with a fork to prevent bubbling.

- Bake in the preheated oven for 15-20 minutes, or until the crust is golden brown. Let it cool completely on a wire rack.
4. **Prepare the Dulce de Leche Filling:**
    - In a medium bowl, beat the heavy cream until soft peaks form.
    - Gently fold in the dulce de leche and vanilla extract until well combined. Be careful not to deflate the whipped cream too much.
5. **Assemble the Tart:**
    - Spread the dulce de leche filling evenly into the cooled tart shell.
    - Smooth the top with a spatula or the back of a spoon.
6. **Chill and Garnish:**
    - Refrigerate the tart for at least 2 hours to allow the filling to set properly.
    - Before serving, garnish with whipped cream, shaved chocolate, cocoa powder, or fresh fruit if desired.
7. **Serve:**
    - Remove the tart from the pan and place it on a serving platter.
    - Slice and serve chilled.

Tips:

- **Dulce de Leche:** If you prefer, you can make your own dulce de leche by simmering a can of sweetened condensed milk, though store-bought is convenient and reliable.
- **Crust Variation:** You can use a pre-made tart shell if you're short on time or prefer a simpler option.
- **Garnishes:** Get creative with garnishes to suit your taste or the occasion. Fresh fruit pairs beautifully with the sweet richness of the tart.

Tarta de Dulce de Leche is a decadent and satisfying dessert that's sure to impress. The combination of buttery tart crust and creamy dulce de leche filling makes it a favorite for many. Enjoy your sweet treat!

Pescado a la Macho

Ingredients:

For the Fish:

- 4 fish fillets (such as tilapia, cod, or sea bass), about 6 oz each
- Salt and black pepper, to taste
- 1 tablespoon all-purpose flour
- 2 tablespoons vegetable oil, for frying

For the Macho Sauce:

- 2 tablespoons vegetable oil
- 1 onion, finely chopped
- 2 cloves garlic, minced
- 1 red bell pepper, chopped
- 1 green bell pepper, chopped
- 1 tablespoon aji amarillo paste (Peruvian yellow chili paste; or substitute with other chili paste or fresh chili)
- 1 tablespoon tomato paste
- 1 cup tomatoes, chopped
- 1 cup fish or chicken stock
- 1/2 cup white wine (optional, can substitute with more stock)
- 1 teaspoon ground cumin
- 1/2 teaspoon paprika
- 1/2 teaspoon dried oregano
- Salt and black pepper, to taste
- 1 tablespoon fresh parsley or cilantro, chopped (for garnish)

Instructions:

1. **Prepare the Fish:**
   - Season the fish fillets with salt and black pepper. Lightly dredge them in flour, shaking off any excess.
   - Heat vegetable oil in a large skillet over medium-high heat. Fry the fish fillets until golden brown and cooked through, about 3-4 minutes per side, depending on thickness. Remove from the skillet and set aside.
2. **Make the Macho Sauce:**
   - In the same skillet, add 2 tablespoons of vegetable oil. Sauté the chopped onion until it becomes translucent, about 3-4 minutes.
   - Add the minced garlic and continue to cook for another 1 minute, until fragrant.

- Stir in the chopped red and green bell peppers and cook for 3-4 minutes until they start to soften.
- Add the aji amarillo paste and tomato paste, stirring to combine and cook for another 2 minutes.
- Add the chopped tomatoes, fish or chicken stock, white wine (if using), ground cumin, paprika, and dried oregano. Stir well and bring the mixture to a simmer. Cook for about 10 minutes, or until the sauce has thickened and the flavors have melded. Adjust seasoning with salt and black pepper.

3. **Combine Fish and Sauce:**
   - Return the fried fish fillets to the skillet with the sauce, spooning the sauce over the fish. Let it simmer for an additional 2-3 minutes to allow the fish to absorb some of the flavors of the sauce.
4. **Serve:**
   - Garnish with fresh parsley or cilantro.
   - Serve the Pescado a la Macho hot, accompanied by white rice, boiled potatoes, or a side of vegetables.

Tips:

- **Aji Amarillo Paste:** If you can't find aji amarillo paste, you can use other types of chili paste or fresh chilies, though they may not provide the exact same flavor.
- **Fish Choice:** Choose firm white fish fillets that hold up well during cooking. Tilapia, cod, and sea bass are all good options.
- **Adjusting Heat:** Adjust the amount of chili paste or fresh chilies to control the heat level according to your preference.

Pescado a la Macho is a robust and hearty dish that brings the flavors of Peruvian cuisine to your table. The spicy, savory sauce perfectly complements the delicate fish, making for a memorable and satisfying meal. Enjoy!

Empanadas de Mariscos

Ingredients:

For the Empanada Dough:

- 3 cups all-purpose flour
- 1 teaspoon salt
- 1/2 teaspoon baking powder
- 1/2 cup unsalted butter, cold and cut into small pieces
- 1 large egg
- 1/2 cup cold water (more if needed)

For the Seafood Filling:

- 1 tablespoon olive oil
- 1 onion, finely chopped
- 2 cloves garlic, minced
- 1 red bell pepper, finely chopped
- 1/2 cup celery, finely chopped
- 1 cup shrimp, peeled, deveined, and chopped
- 1 cup crab meat (or additional shrimp, or a mix of seafood)
- 1/2 cup fish fillet, diced (optional)
- 1/4 cup fresh parsley, chopped
- 1/4 cup fresh cilantro, chopped (optional)
- 1/2 teaspoon paprika
- 1/2 teaspoon ground cumin
- 1/4 teaspoon dried oregano
- Salt and black pepper, to taste
- 1/4 cup heavy cream or milk (optional, for creaminess)
- 1 egg, beaten (for egg wash)

Instructions:

1. **Prepare the Empanada Dough:**
    - In a large bowl, whisk together the flour, salt, and baking powder.
    - Cut in the cold butter using a pastry cutter or your fingers until the mixture resembles coarse crumbs.
    - In a small bowl, beat the egg and mix with the cold water. Gradually add this to the flour mixture, stirring until a dough forms. Add more water, a tablespoon at a time, if the dough is too dry.
    - Knead the dough lightly on a floured surface until smooth. Wrap in plastic wrap and refrigerate for at least 30 minutes.

2. **Prepare the Seafood Filling:**
   - Heat olive oil in a large skillet over medium heat. Sauté the onion and garlic until softened, about 3-4 minutes.
   - Add the red bell pepper and celery, and cook for another 3-4 minutes.
   - Add the shrimp, crab meat, and fish (if using). Cook until the shrimp are pink and the fish is cooked through, about 3-5 minutes. Be careful not to overcook.
   - Stir in the parsley, cilantro (if using), paprika, cumin, oregano, salt, and black pepper. If desired, add the heavy cream or milk for extra creaminess. Cook for another 1-2 minutes to combine.
   - Remove from heat and let the filling cool.
3. **Assemble the Empanadas:**
   - Preheat your oven to 375°F (190°C) and line a baking sheet with parchment paper.
   - On a floured surface, roll out the dough to about 1/8-inch thickness. Cut into circles using a cookie cutter or a glass (about 4-5 inches in diameter).
   - Place a tablespoon of the seafood filling in the center of each dough circle. Fold the dough over to form a half-moon shape and crimp the edges to seal. You can use a fork to press the edges together or fold and pinch the edges for a traditional look.
   - Place the empanadas on the prepared baking sheet and brush the tops with the beaten egg for a golden finish.
4. **Bake:**
   - Bake in the preheated oven for 20-25 minutes, or until the empanadas are golden brown and crisp.
5. **Serve:**
   - Allow the empanadas to cool slightly before serving. They are delicious warm or at room temperature.

Tips:

- **Dough:** If you prefer, you can use store-bought empanada dough to save time.
- **Filling Variations:** Feel free to customize the filling with other seafood like scallops or mussels, or add vegetables like corn or peas.
- **Freezing:** You can freeze assembled empanadas before baking. Just place them on a baking sheet, freeze until solid, and then transfer to a freezer bag. Bake from frozen, adding a few extra minutes to the cooking time.

Empanadas de Mariscos are a delightful and versatile dish that can be enjoyed as a snack, appetizer, or main course. The combination of savory seafood and crispy pastry is always a hit. Enjoy your homemade empanadas!

Fideos con Salsa de Tomate

Ingredients:

For the Pasta:

- 250 g (about 8 oz) pasta (spaghetti, elbow macaroni, or your preferred type)
- Salt (to taste)
- Water (for boiling)

For the Tomato Sauce:

- 4 large ripe tomatoes (or you can use canned tomatoes)
- 1 large onion, finely chopped
- 2 garlic cloves, minced
- 2 tablespoons olive oil or vegetable oil
- 1 teaspoon sugar (optional, to balance the acidity)
- 1 teaspoon dried oregano
- 1/2 teaspoon dried or fresh basil (if available)
- Salt and pepper to taste
- 1/2 cup water or vegetable broth (if needed)
- 1 red bell pepper (optional, finely chopped)
- 1 small carrot (optional, finely chopped)

Instructions:

Prepare the Pasta:

1. **Boil the Water:** Fill a large pot with water and add a pinch of salt. Bring to a boil.
2. **Cook the Pasta:** Once the water is boiling, add the pasta and cook according to the package instructions, usually 8 to 12 minutes, until al dente.
3. **Drain:** Drain the pasta and set aside.

Prepare the Tomato Sauce:

1. **Prepare the Tomatoes:** If using fresh tomatoes, make a small cross-cut at the base of each tomato and immerse them in boiling water for about 30 seconds. Then transfer them to a bowl of cold water. This helps to peel them easily. Peel the tomatoes and chop them into small cubes.
2. **Sauté the Ingredients:** In a large skillet, heat the oil over medium heat. Add the onion and bell pepper (if using) and cook until the onion is translucent, about 5 minutes. Add the garlic and cook for another minute.

3. **Add the Tomatoes:** Add the chopped tomatoes, carrot (if using), oregano, basil, and sugar. Cook over medium-low heat for about 15-20 minutes, stirring occasionally, until the tomatoes break down and the sauce thickens. If the sauce becomes too thick, add a bit of water or broth.
4. **Season:** Adjust the seasoning with salt and pepper to taste.

Mix and Serve:

1. **Combine:** Add the drained pasta to the sauce and mix well to coat the pasta with the sauce.
2. **Serve:** Serve hot. You can top with grated cheese or fresh parsley if desired.

And there you have it—a delicious plate of pasta with tomato sauce, Chilean style. Enjoy!

Lentejas con Chorizo

Ingredients

- 1 cup dried lentils (green or brown, rinsed and drained)
- 200g (7 oz) chorizo sausage, sliced (you can use Spanish chorizo or a good quality one)
- 1 onion, finely chopped
- 2 cloves garlic, minced
- 1 bell pepper, chopped (red or green)
- 2 carrots, peeled and diced
- 2 tomatoes, diced (or one 14.5 oz can of diced tomatoes)
- 1 potato, peeled and diced
- 1 bay leaf
- 1 tsp smoked paprika
- 1 tsp ground cumin (optional)
- 1 tsp dried thyme (optional)
- 4 cups chicken or vegetable broth
- 2 tbsp olive oil
- Salt and black pepper, to taste

Instructions

1. **Prep the Lentils:**
    - Rinse the lentils under cold water and set them aside.
2. **Cook the Chorizo:**
    - In a large pot or Dutch oven, heat 1 tablespoon of olive oil over medium heat.
    - Add the sliced chorizo and cook until it starts to brown and release its oils. Remove the chorizo from the pot and set it aside.
3. **Sauté the Vegetables:**
    - In the same pot, add the remaining tablespoon of olive oil.
    - Add the chopped onion, garlic, and bell pepper. Sauté until the onion is translucent and the bell pepper is tender, about 5 minutes.
    - Stir in the diced carrots and cook for an additional 5 minutes.
4. **Add the Tomatoes and Spices:**
    - Add the diced tomatoes (or canned tomatoes) to the pot.
    - Stir in the smoked paprika, cumin (if using), thyme (if using), and bay leaf. Cook for a couple of minutes until the tomatoes start to break down.
5. **Combine and Simmer:**
    - Return the chorizo to the pot and add the lentils, diced potato, and broth.
    - Bring the mixture to a boil, then reduce the heat to low. Cover and simmer for about 30-40 minutes, or until the lentils and potatoes are tender. Stir occasionally and check the seasoning, adding salt and pepper to taste.

6. **Serve:**
    - Remove the bay leaf before serving.
    - Serve the lentjas con chorizo hot, garnished with fresh parsley if desired. It pairs well with crusty bread.

Enjoy your comforting and flavorful Spanish stew!

Pan de Trigo

Ingredients

- 4 cups all-purpose flour (plus extra for dusting)
- 1 1/2 cups warm water (110°F or 45°C)
- 2 1/4 tsp active dry yeast (1 packet)
- 2 tbsp sugar
- 2 tbsp olive oil (or any vegetable oil)
- 1 1/2 tsp salt

Instructions

1. **Activate the Yeast:**
    - In a small bowl, combine the warm water and sugar. Sprinkle the yeast over the top and let it sit for about 5-10 minutes, until it becomes frothy.
2. **Mix the Dough:**
    - In a large mixing bowl, combine 3 cups of flour and the salt.
    - Make a well in the center and pour in the yeast mixture and olive oil.
    - Stir until the mixture begins to come together. Gradually add the remaining flour, a little at a time, until a soft dough forms.
3. **Knead the Dough:**
    - Turn the dough onto a floured surface and knead for about 8-10 minutes, until the dough is smooth and elastic. Add more flour if the dough is too sticky.
4. **First Rise:**
    - Lightly oil a large bowl and place the dough inside, turning it around to coat it with oil.
    - Cover the bowl with a clean, damp cloth or plastic wrap and let it rise in a warm, draft-free area for about 1 to 1.5 hours, or until it has doubled in size.
5. **Shape the Bread:**
    - Once the dough has risen, punch it down to release the air. Turn it out onto a floured surface and shape it into a loaf.
    - Place the shaped dough into a greased loaf pan or onto a parchment-lined baking sheet.
6. **Second Rise:**
    - Cover the loaf with a cloth and let it rise again for about 30 minutes, or until it has puffed up.
7. **Bake:**
    - Preheat your oven to 375°F (190°C).
    - Bake the bread for 25-30 minutes, or until the loaf sounds hollow when tapped on the bottom and has a golden-brown crust.
8. **Cool:**

- Remove the bread from the oven and let it cool on a wire rack before slicing.

Tips

- For a softer crust, you can brush the top of the loaf with melted butter before baking.
- If you like a crustier bread, you can place a small pan of water on the bottom rack of the oven to create steam during baking.

Enjoy your freshly baked Pan de Trigo with butter, jams, or your favorite sandwich fillings!

Arrollado de Huaso

Ingredients

- 2.5 to 3 pounds (1.1 to 1.4 kg) pork shoulder or pork loin, trimmed of excess fat
- 4 cloves garlic, minced
- 2 tbsp paprika
- 1 tbsp ground cumin
- 1 tbsp dried oregano
- 1 tbsp ground black pepper
- 2 tsp salt (or to taste)
- 1/4 cup olive oil
- 1/2 cup white wine (or chicken broth)
- 2 tbsp fresh parsley, chopped (optional, for garnish)

Instructions

1. **Prepare the Pork:**
   - Place the pork shoulder or loin on a clean surface. Using a sharp knife, carefully trim any excess fat, but leave a thin layer for flavor and moisture.
2. **Season the Pork:**
   - In a small bowl, mix the minced garlic, paprika, cumin, oregano, black pepper, and salt.
   - Rub this seasoning mixture all over the pork, making sure it is evenly coated. If you have time, let it marinate in the refrigerator for a few hours or overnight for deeper flavor.
3. **Roll the Pork:**
   - Roll the pork tightly into a log shape, securing it with kitchen twine. Tie the twine at intervals along the length of the roll to keep it together during cooking.
4. **Sear the Pork:**
   - Preheat your oven to 350°F (175°C).
   - Heat the olive oil in a large oven-safe skillet or roasting pan over medium-high heat.
   - Sear the pork roll on all sides until it is browned and crispy, about 3-4 minutes per side.
5. **Roast the Pork:**
   - Once the pork is seared, remove it from the skillet and set it aside.
   - Deglaze the skillet with the white wine or chicken broth, scraping up any browned bits from the bottom of the pan.
   - Return the pork to the skillet or roasting pan, placing it on top of the deglazed liquid.
   - Cover the skillet or pan with aluminum foil and place it in the preheated oven.

6. **Cook:**
   - Roast the pork for about 1.5 to 2 hours, or until the internal temperature reaches 145°F (63°C) and the meat is tender. Baste occasionally with the pan juices to keep it moist.
7. **Rest and Slice:**
   - Remove the pork from the oven and let it rest for about 15 minutes before slicing. This helps the juices redistribute and makes slicing easier.
   - Remove the twine before serving.
8. **Serve:**
   - Slice the Arrollado de Huaso into thick slices and serve with your favorite sides. It's often enjoyed with Chilean sides like pebre, roasted vegetables, or a fresh salad.

Tips

- **Marinating:** For the best flavor, allow the pork to marinate with the spices for at least a few hours or overnight.
- **Basting:** Keep an eye on the pork while it's roasting. If the pan juices evaporate, you can add a bit more wine or broth to keep it from drying out.

Enjoy your delicious Arrollado de Huaso!

www.ingramcontent.com/pod-product-compliance
Lightning Source LLC
LaVergne TN
LVHW081603060526
838201LV00054B/2056